DOUBLE VISION

DOUBLE VISION

Asian Accounts of Australia

Edited by
Alison Broinowski

E PRESS

Published by ANU E Press
The Australian National University
Canberra ACT 0200, Australia
Email: anuepress@anu.edu.au
This title is also available online at: http://epress.anu.edu.au/

National Library of Australia Cataloguing-in-Publication entry

ISBN 9781921862267 (pbk.) 9781921862274 (ebook)

Subjects: Australia--Foreign public opinion, Asian.
            Asia--Foreign relations--Australia.
            Australia--Foreign relations--Asia.

Other Authors/Contributors:
            Broinowski, Alison.

Dewey Number: 327.5094

All rights reserved. No part of this publication may be reproduced, stored in a retrieval system or transmitted in any form or by any means, electronic, mechanical, photocopying or otherwise, without the prior permission of the publisher.

Printed by Griffin Press
This edition © 2011 ANU E Press
First edition © 2004 Pandanus Books

In memory of John Woodroffe, 1918–2003

CONTENTS

Introduction   1
   Alison Broinowski and Anthony Milner

East Asian Perceptions of Australia   11
   Kevin Rudd

CHINA

1. Who Cares *What* They Think? John Winston   15
   Howard, William Morris Hughes and the Pragmatic
   Vision of Australian National Sovereignty
      John Fitzgerald

2. 'Before we came to this country, we heard that   41
   English laws were good and kind to everybody':
   Chinese Immigrants' Views of Colonial Australia
      Paul Macgregor

3. Australian Lovers: Chingchong Chinaman,   61
   Chinese Identity and Hybrid Confusion
      Kam Louie

4. *Haigui*: A Keyword for 2003 79
   Ouyang Yu

JAPAN

5. Murakami Haruki's *Sydney Diary* 93
   Leith Morton

6. *Tampa* in Japan: East Asian Responses 105
   to Australia's Refugee Policy
   Tessa Morris-Suzuki

7. 'Japanese' Accounts of Australia: A Player's View 123
   Yoshio Sugimoto

8. Reading Japanese Reflections of Australia 131
   Masayo Tada

AUSTRALIA AND ASIA

9. Asian Australian Studies in Asia: China and Japan 139
   David Carter

10. Australia as Model or Moral 155
    Alison Broinowski

Note: Chinese and Japanese names are given with the family name first, except where the person named reverses the order.

CONTRIBUTORS

Dr Alison Broinowski, Faculty of Asian Studies, ANU

Associate Professor David Carter, University of Queensland

Professor John Fitzgerald, La Trobe University

Professor Kam Louie, Faculty of Asian Studies, ANU

Paul Macgregor, Curator, Chinese Museum, Melbourne

Professor Anthony Milner, Faculty of Asian Studies, ANU

Professor Tessa Morris-Suzuki, Research School of Pacific and Asian Studies, ANU

Professor Leith Morton, University of Newcastle

Dr Ouyang Yu, Author and Editor, Melbourne

Kevin Rudd, MP, Opposition Spokesman for Foreign Affairs

Professor Yoshio Sugimoto, La Trobe University

Dr Masayo Tada, ANU

INTRODUCTION

Alison Broinowski and Anthony Milner

Chinese, Japanese and Australians have shared an intense curiosity about each other throughout our recorded histories. As is well known, settlers from Europe brought with them to Australia preconceptions about China and Japan, some fanciful, some factual. Some convicts, believing they had been transported almost to China itself, hoped that by escaping from the penal settlements on the east coast of Australia and walking north they would reach China. Others set out in boats and some got to Batavia, while others reached the coast of Japan. What is less widely known is that their curiosity was matched by early investigations of Australia by Chinese and Japanese, which some Chinese claim began in the 15th century. Certainly, small teams of diligent Japanese followed them in the 19th century. The process of mutual exploration continues into the 21st century.

The examination of how Australia is perceived by people from the Asian region is important, yet it remains a much neglected project.[1] To investigate how Australia appears from other points of view, and particularly those of people in two such significant societies, is to challenge Australian self-perceptions. Equally, from Chinese and Japanese reports about Australia emerge interesting suggestions about how the Chinese and Japanese observe themselves. In what Chinese and

Japanese say about Australia, curiosity about difference and the impulse to compare are as potent as in Australian accounts of them. So in this investigation a kind of double vision is at work, juxtaposing two sets of images and three societies.

We asked the distinguished contributors to this book to select examples, from their knowledge of Chinese or Japanese sources, of accounts of Australia, to analyse them in their cultural context and to draw conclusions about how Australia is perceived among Chinese and Japanese. We asked them to take account of the Chinese- and Japanese-language material that our researchers had identified and translated in the 'Australiana' collections of the National Library of Australia as part of the 'Asian Accounts of Australia' project, the pilot phase of which began in 1999. The results were presented to the public at a conference on 6 February, 2003 at the National Library of Australia, which marked the end of the project. This book is an edited collection of the papers. By publishing them we hope to make the National Library's wealth of Chinese and Japanese Australiana more widely accessible, for linguists and non-linguists. More information about the project's findings can be found on the National Library's web site.

Our researchers, graduate students in Chinese and Japanese from the Australian National University, selected and categorised the material, comprising thousands of items, under several headings:

— Australia as a place of settlement and invasion;
— Australia as exotic and a place for tourism;
— Australia as a model and a place for education;
— Australia as a political entity and a regional participant;
— Cultural Australia;
— Indigenous Australia, racist Australia and multicultural Australia;
— Republican Australia;
— Sydney Olympic Games.

Some of these fields, which were identified in the pilot project in 1999, turned out to be more fertile for our purposes than others. Australia is important as a participant in East

Asian commercial affairs, for instance, but the Chinese and Japanese accounts of this aspect of Australia, being necessarily factual, contributed less of perceptual interest to the project than those on other topics. As a model country, Australia was seen by some Chinese and Japanese observers as setting an example in some respects, but these accounts were rarely without their down-side, and most included warnings that the Australian way was far from perfect. We detected in some accounts an almost conspiratorial tone, as though Chinese and Japanese were passing on home truths about Australia to readers of the vernacular which, if they were writing in English, they might have been more circumspect in expressing. We learned from our research not to try to anticipate how others may see us, since by doing so the very categories we set may distort what the material has to tell us.

An impression left with us by the project is how enduring early impressions of Australia remain among Chinese and Japanese. Many descriptions are so similar they seem either to have been based on the same sources or to result from preconceptions that existed even before the observers arrived in Australia, and which were readily confirmed by what they saw. It seems almost obligatory to affirm readers' expectations by commenting on Australia's Westernness or Britishness, its small population, wide open spaces, agriculture, exotic animals and the leisured lifestyle of Australians, before getting down to anything more original. We were surprised by the large number of encyclopaedic, survey-style accounts of Australia for Chinese readers that provide broadly similar outlines of Australian history, politics and society. As well, multiple handbooks instruct Chinese about migration, settlement, education and the social welfare system. In Japanese, accounts of women's experiences in Australia are almost as numerous as studies of Aboriginal communities, and both categories include firsthand experiences of Japanese who have lived in Australia for extended periods, either in cities or in the outback.

More surprises were in store for us when we read an account of 327 Chinese who were shipwrecked off what is now

Papua New Guinea in 1858 on their way to Australia. According to the Chinese writer, they were captured by local tribespeople who fattened them up for months before killing and eating all but three of them. Equally dramatic is the Japanese attack on Sydney Harbour in 1942 and the experiences of the crew of the three midget submarines. Another Japanese wartime account of Australia in 1944 describes Australians' reputation for violence, arguing that it derives from their being accustomed as children to killing animals, using guns and training wild horses, as well as the fact that they are the descendants of convicts. For these writers, for different reasons, Australia is a remote, dangerous, frontier place, which East Asians enter at their peril.

Closer to the present, Chinese observers of Australia often have comparisons with China in mind. One of them in 1999 describes the relaxed and comfortable atmosphere of visiting time at 'Long Beach prison' (Long Bay Jail), and calls it 'a really nice place'. But three years earlier, a Chinese man with a medical degree who is working as an orderly in a geriatric hospital is sworn at in the street: 'Bloody stupid Chinese go home!' He reflects bitterly that he is caring for the parents of these rude people, while the elderly are looked after at home in China. Variations appear between mainland, Hong Kong and Taiwanese observations of Australia, with the latter often reporting more positive experiences. A satire from a Hong Kong newspaper in 1997, however, comments on how little work is done in Australia during the week, because it is squeezed between the overriding demands of the weekend.

Similar comments about Australian laziness and inefficiency are recurrent in Japanese accounts of Australia where, according to some business people, the serious work of the day is done after 5pm. But these observations about the way Australians divide their time between work and leisure, together with commentaries on the relative autonomy of Australian schoolchildren, and the comparative equality of gender roles, reflect long-standing concern in Japan about rigidities in their society and about lifetimes of hard work that may not be fulfilling, no matter how sophisticated the possessions they deliver.

While long-standing patterns of perception exist in texts in both languages, and remain powerfully influential, it is at times when those images undergo revision that we have the most to learn about Chinese and Japanese accounts of Australia. Such moments of change are discussed by several of the contributors to this book. They are leading scholars in their fields of Chinese studies, Japanese studies and Australian studies. They include associate researchers who have worked with the project since 1999. Included in the collection is the opening address to the conference given by the Opposition Spokesman for Foreign Affairs, himself a scholar of Chinese.

In their famous pamphlet of 1879, *The Chinese Question*, prominent Chinese residents of Melbourne put their case for equal treatment with other migrants to Australia. They compared starving and over-populated China with prosperous Australia and argued that the same Christian and Confucian principles, of treating others as you would be treated, should apply to all God's children. As Paul Macgregor shows in Chapter 3, their claims to be model citizens were founded on the unspoken premise that Chinese civilisation was superior, which made the injustice done to them in Australia even greater. More than a century later, some echoes of these views, but also marked changes, are noticed by Kam Louie. In Chapter 4, he reviews Chinese fiction written by post-Tienanmen students and their successors. All are enthusiastic supporters of Australian multiculturalism, and all aspire to Permanent Residency as their new identity. Many are prepared to enter into complex mating strategies to get it. Some succeed, yet others are as disappointed in their hopes for a new identity in Australia as were their sojourner predecessors. Ouyang Yu updates this further, describing in Chapter 8 how Chinese abroad who have Permanent Residency are now being wooed back to China by attractive job offers. Chinese leaving Australia say it's quiet and dull, with blue sky, clean air and nothing else: a place for old people. So for Ouyang, the latest and greatest change is that many Chinese, once pushed back by the West, are now being pulled back by a vibrant, dynamic, prosperous China where their talents are better appreciated.

An immature, derivative culture, which has borrowed its civilisation from Britain and America, is how Chinese frequently observe Australia. But in the decades in which Kevin Rudd has observed China, he has seen that change twice. Australia came to be seen by Chinese in the late 20th century as taking the region seriously and as trying to build Asia literacy to enhance its place there, even if Chinese suspected that Australians were still fearful of the growing power of East Asia and were opportunistically eager to take advantage of East Asian growth. Then, as a result of Prime Minister John Howard's explicit association of Australia with United States policy, even to the point of threatening pre-emptively to strike against suspected terrorists in the region, a powerful impression has been created among Chinese that Australia has abandoned an appropriate view of its role and status. Perceptions, Rudd warns in Chapter 1, shape behaviour, and changed Chinese impressions of Australia will be hard to wind back.

Approaching China historically, John Fitzgerald in Chapter 2 finds word-for-word echoes of Prime Minister William Morris Hughes in Howard's pronouncements on refugees and asylum-seekers, and more resonances in his pragmatic, xenophobic interpretation of the national interest. Australians alone, said Hughes, would decide who 'should enter in' to this country. Australians, says Howard, will decide who comes into this country and the circumstances under which they come. Hughes' notoriety was much greater in Japan than in China, where little was known about Australia beyond the long-standing view that it was a convict colony, a police state and a lackey of the US. Yet as Fitzgerald proposes, the collapse in 1919 of the Chinese republic, the cession of Shantung to Japan and China's turn toward communism were all outcomes of

Australia's blocking of racial equality in the League of Nations. Seventy years later, what a change! Equipped as many Chinese now are with wide Internet access to accurate information about Australia, they often ask about Pauline Hanson and the 'new' racism, and Australia's anti-migration policies. They want to know why Australia's assertion of sovereignty over its borders is not matched by a desire to 'stand up' (as Mao said of China) for its own Head of State. An impression derived from China's own preoccupations as much as from fact, which has not changed, is of Australia's lack of maturity and independence.

Leith Morton has read a diary written by a famous Japanese author/journalist during three weeks in Australia at the time of the 2000 Olympic Games. He finds in Chapter 5 that Haruki Murakami, like modern observers in China, researched Australian history and society from the copious, electronically available information as well as from standard sources and the daily press. These inform Murakami's observations about anti-Aboriginal racism, stolen indigenous children and Australia's propensity to fight for Britain and America in war after war. Unlike the Chinese, who remark on Australia's neatness and cleanliness, however, he comments on the crumbling, faded Sydney suburbs he sees on the way to Parramatta. Rather than the orderliness on which Chinese often remark in Australia, the criminal tendencies of Australians, resulting from their convict ancestry, are confirmed for Murakami by the theft of his expensive laptop computer from his hotel room. Like the Chinese, Murakami notices a change: for him, it is a new Australian assertiveness, which he sees as being officially encouraged in the Olympic crowds in order to displace Australians' guilt for their convict past and for their discrimination against Aborigines — and he finds it irritating.

Yoshio Sugimoto, who, like his wife Machiko Satō, has written and broadcast many commentaries on Australia from the viewpoint of Japanese for some 30 years, is a contributor to as well as an analyst of perceptions of Australia in Japan. But he says in Chapter 7 that the segment of the Japanese audience with an interest in Australia remains small. Two assumptions are widespread among them: that Japanese business people are more stressed and tense than Australians, and that Japanese society is less multicultural than Australia. These are among the considerations documented by Machiko Satō that lead Japanese 'lifestyle migrants', particularly women, to migrate to Australia. Masayo Tada further divides gender-related perceptions of Australia in Chapter 9 into three groups: Japanese businessmen, who pity and scorn the uxorious 'Australian husband'; married women, who generally prefer the educational practices and gender equality in Australia to those in Japan; and single mothers, for whom Australia provides comparative liberation. But Sugimoto draws attention to the change in Australia since 1996. As a result of Hanson, the *Tampa* affair and Australia's support of the attack on Iraq, he says Japanese no longer see Australia as a successful multicultural society. Questions are asked about whether Australians are now a militaristic people, more so than Japanese.

Even though she agrees that Australian affairs are not widely reported in East Asian capitals, Tessa Morris-Suzuki observes in Chapter 6 that refugee and asylum-seeker policy has been more intensively covered in Japan than the Hanson issue was. In spite of the fact that Japan, like most countries in the region, seeks to exclude refugees, Japanese have in the past admired Australia's success in accepting them, and the reformist press has used Australia's example to press for change in Japan. The *Tampa* episode was at first reported blandly and briefly, but then the Government's 'Pacific Solution' and the efforts of Melbourne lawyers to oppose it were widely discussed in the Japanese media. This brought about another change: the *Asahi Shimbun* wrote that tolerant Australia, which took in many more Indo-Chinese refugees than Japan, had been transformed, and that attitudes were hardening in Australia and elsewhere. Australia, as a counter-model for Japan, is now seen by several commentators to be losing the esteem it once had.

The research that led to these papers and this book proves, if it was in any doubt, that perceptions are powerful in the way societies respond to each other. Long-established images may be in need of change, but when they change, it may not always be for the betterment of Australia's reputation. Australia has opportunities to be admired and even influential in China and Japan; because of recent changes in Australian behaviour we appear to be squandering them. Behaviour is one side of our image problem; projection is the other. In Chapter 10, David Carter argues the case for more and better Australian cultural diplomacy in China and Japan and, in particular, for the gaps in Australian studies abroad to be filled. A country that does not appear to care whether its history is well known or its culture admired risks diminishing such influence as it has in China and Japan. Plenty of other small and medium-sized countries are competing to have their voices heard there, and if Australian studies are not invigorated and promoted as part of a coordinated image-improvement strategy, Australia's small voice will easily be shouted down.

The project team expresses its appreciation to Vice-Chancellor Ian Chubb of The Australian National University and, in particular, to our team leaders, Professor Anthony Milner and Professor Mark Finnane. Griffith University funded the 1999 pilot project and we are grateful to Professor Finnane for that and for his continuous support of our researchers. We acknowledge with appreciation the grant from the Australian Research Council and the matching assistance from the National Library of Australia that made our research possible. Chief investigators were Shun Ikeda (ANU) and Dr Alison Broinowski; our associate researchers were Professor Mark Elvin (ANU), Professor John Fitzgerald (Latrobe University) and Associate Professor David Carter (University of Queensland). At the National Library, we had unfailing cooperation from the director, Jan Fullerton, and from Pam Gatenby, Marie Sexton, Andrew Gosling, Heather Clark and the dedicated staff of the Asian Collections.

The backbone and nerve centre of the project were its research associates, administrators and translators. Graduate students from ANU who worked on Chinese material were Nicole Mies, Christine Eckhardt, Thomas Kwok, Ines Rittgasser and Lynn Xiaoling Li. Those who worked on Japanese material were Meredith Box, Peter Trebilco, Keiko Yamada Foster, Manabu Kawakatsu, Steven Bullard, Tomoko Dorman, Ben Dorman and Adam Broinowski. Our successive project administrators who kept the operation moving were Ruth Barraclough, Judy Laffan, Rosie Smith and Nguyet Barraclough, ably supported by the staff of the Faculty of Asian Studies at ANU.

Footnote

1. Considerable scholarly research investigates the way the immigrant Australian population has responded over time to living in close proximity to the Asian region. See, for instance, Walker, David. 1999. *Anxious Nation*. St Lucia, Queensland: University of Queensland Press. Walker, David (ed.). 1990. Australian Perceptions of Asia. *Australian Cultural History No.9*. Broinowski, Alison. 1992, 1996. *The Yellow Lady: Australian Impressions of Asia*. South Melbourne: Oxford University Press. Sheridan, Greg (ed.). 1995. *Living with Dragons: Australia Confronts its Asian Destiny*. Sydney: Allen & Unwin. D'Cruz, J.V. and William Steele. 2000. *Australia's Ambivalence Towards Asia: Politics, Neo/Post-Colonialism and Fact/Fiction*. Kuala Lumpur: Malaysian Book Publishers Association. McGillivray, Mark and Gary Smith (eds). 1997. *Australia and Asia*. South Melbourne: Oxford University Press. Dobell, Graeme. 2000. *Australia Finds Home: The choices and chances of an Asian Pacific journey*. Sydney: Australian Broadcasting Association. FitzGerald, Stephen. 1997. *Is Australia an Asian Country?* Sydney: Allen & Unwin. Garnaut, Ross. 1989. *Australia and the Northeast Asian Ascendancy*. Canberra: Australian Government Publishing Service. The last two books give exploratory consideration to Asian 'perceptions of Australia'. See Garnaut's Chapter 16: Australia and Northeast Asia in Each Other's Minds. The Academy of the Social Sciences' Australian-Asian Perceptions Project compared the value and conceptual systems operating in Australia with those encountered in a range of Asian societies. Although this research threw light on the way many people from Asian societies perceived Australia, it did not focus specifically on Asian accounts of Australia. Its results appeared in Milner, Anthony and Mar Quilty (eds), 1996, *Australia in Asia: Comparing Cultures*. South Melbourne: Oxford University Press. And Milner, Anthony. 1996. Defining Australia in Asia. In Jones, Gavin (ed.), 1996, *Australia and its Asian Context: Cunningham Lecture and Symposium 1995*. Canberra: Academy of the Social Sciences in Australia. A specific examination of Indonesian perceptions of Australia (in Indonesian) is Chauvel, Richard, Philip Kitley and David Reeve. 1989. *Australia di Mata Indonesia*. Jakarta: Penerbit PT Gramedia. Translation and analysis from the 'Asian Accounts of Australia Project' (on which the present volume is based) are contained in a doctoral thesis by Broinowski, Alison, 2001, About Face: Asian representations of Australia. ANU, doctoral thesis. And Broinowski, Alison. 2003. *About Face: Asian Accounts of Australia*. Carlton, Victoria: Scribe. The latter seeks to address the neglect of the examination of how Australia is perceived in the Asian region.

EAST ASIAN PERCEPTIONS OF AUSTRALIA

Kevin Rudd

My experience of Asia has been shaped largely by the experience of studying Chinese and working as a diplomat in China. There I was struck by the importance of mutual perceptions between China and Australia, and China and the West.

The Chinese devote much effort to understanding the Western — or, most commonly, the American — mind and how it works in business. But I was also impressed with the widespread reverence among Chinese for antiquity and continuity, something they see Australia as lacking.

For decades, scholars in Asian studies in Australia have been working to get other Australians to appreciate the necessity of improving our knowledge of our neighbours' languages and cultures: indeed, there have been 16 or 17 reports on Asian studies in Australia since the 1960s.

In East Asian societies, perceptions of Australia have their roots in the distant past, in folklore and tradition. For many in those countries, their first contact with Australians was with missionaries, who typically saw Asia as an 'ocean of souls' to be 'fished'.

Australia was widely associated with white Western colonialism and, as a result of promotion of the White Australia Policy, its defining characteristic in the region for more than a century became whiteness itself. The long-term impact of that period remains with us.

Australia is commonly perceived in East Asian countries as having a derivative culture: a mixture of British and American. To the extent that we are seen as taking the Asian region seriously, it is often assumed that we do so for two reasons: because Australia fears the rising power of Asia and because Asian countries offer Australians opportunities to make money.

Even before the negative developments of recent years in Australia's relations with Asian countries, there was an underlying cynicism about Australia's motives for increasing its engagement with the region. Now, that feeling has been compounded by the perception that Australia is abandoning those efforts, and reforms that began with the abolition of the White Australia Policy in the late 1960s appear to have been wound back.

The latest perception problems began with the rise of 'Hansonism' and the Howard Government's partial embrace of One Nation's policies. The evidence of the damage that episode did to perceptions of Australia in the minds of East Asian people is quite conclusive.

Then came the Howard Doctrine Mark I, which asserted a role for Australia in East Asia as the 'deputy sheriff' to the United States. Although this had a short life among issues of public concern in Australia, it has been run and re-run at conferences and in the editorial pages of newspapers in East Asia for the past three years.

As well, we now have Howard Doctrine Mark II, by which, in the name of regional military pre-emption, the Government reserves the right to launch a strike against a sovereign state in the region if it judges it necessary in pursuit of its anti-terrorism objectives.

Whatever merit pre-emption may have as an internal operations policy, as an external policy of any government it has none. It has created a powerful, negative impression of Australia in the region, and has confirmed in the minds of many in East Asian countries that Australia is reverting to becoming anti-Asian.

This is significant because perceptions shape behaviour, and the perceptions of Australia among the politicians and business people in East Asian countries condition their dealings with us. Thus the way we prosecute our interests is endangered, but so too is our self-image as Australians.

The growth of an Asia-literate Australia has been appreciated in the region — and if we continue to learn Asian languages and study Asian cultures that appreciation will grow.

Australians should, however, develop an appropriate form of national modesty, which enables us in our dealings with people in East Asian societies to avoid being over the top or grossly humble. Only by doing so can we hope to undo the damage that has recently been done to perceptions of Australia in the region.

1. WHO CARES *WHAT* THEY THINK? JOHN WINSTON HOWARD, WILLIAM MORRIS HUGHES AND THE PRAGMATIC VISION OF AUSTRALIAN NATIONAL SOVEREIGNTY

John Fitzgerald

Introduction
What others think about Australia matters to Australians. Their sensitivity on this point is often playfully mocked in stories about journalists accosting visiting celebrities as they step off the plane and asking what they think about the country. But there is nothing playful about the response of Australians when they don't like what they hear. Musician Bob Dylan was asked what he thought of Australia as soon as he alighted at Sydney airport in April 1966, and was asked the same question again a week later when he flew into Melbourne. His blunt critique and trademark ironies were not well received. One miffed journalist warned Dylan that he had 'better be careful' what he said about Australia.[1]

Australian governments are equally sensitive to world opinion. In a foreign-policy address to the Sydney Institute in July 2003, Prime Minister John Howard congratulated his government for earning 'unparalleled world respect' for its stand on terrorism. This was not an ill-considered remark. Australia had played a supportive role in the Iraq war. But even before the outbreak of war in Iraq, Howard claimed on several occasions that Australia's international reputation had reached unprecedentedly high levels under his administration.[2] Australia's standing in the opinion of others matters as much to national leaders today as it did to airport journalists back in 1966.

World opinion is an elusive creature. To the best of my knowledge there are no systematic surveys of Australia's current standing in the world, country by country, comparable with the Pew Global Attitudes Project which publishes half-yearly surveys of international impressions of the US and the standing of the US President. In the absence of reliable survey data, Australians have little choice but to fall back on their impressions of others' impressions of themselves. My impression is that Australia's standing in the Asian region has deteriorated rather than improved in recent years, much as the Pew Survey reveals the US image to have deteriorated in the Muslim world during the same period.[3] This impression is open to correction.[4] But what appears beyond dispute is the growing indifference of Australia's governing élite to the views of Asian leaders and opinion-makers in their calculation of 'world opinion'. The world opinion to which Howard refers seems to exclude the opinion of people and governments in East, South and South-East Asia, as well as 'old Europe' and possibly much of Africa and Latin America. Perhaps Australia's leaders don't like what they hear in the region, but their indifference has dangerous precedents.

Personal anecdotes and impressions offer no substitute for systematic surveys but they do help to frame questions for historical reflection. This chapter draws upon anecdotal impressions of Chinese impressions of Australia to frame questions about Australia that do not often arise when Australians reflect simply upon themselves.

Impressions of impressions

My earliest personal encounter with a Maoist impression of Australia dates to the first industrial exhibition staged by the People's Republic of China in Australia, at the Sydney Showgrounds, in 1974. A student of Sydney University at the time, I struck up a conversation with a visiting lathe operator who stood guard over the pride of Shanghai industry of the day, huge leaden generators arrayed among stands of olive-green lathes and electric motors. 'What do you think of Australia?' I asked. He shot back immediately: 'Australia is a police state.' Things could only improve.

In Mao's day, Australia was counted a repressive police state at home and a lackey of US imperialism abroad. Such impressions were easily created and maintained through strict control of information flows that still held sway in the late Mao era. But things were changing even then. I recall standing around the TV room in a Chinese university three years later watching a television program about Sydney Harbour. For me it evoked familiar crisp mornings spent delivering newspapers around Milson's Point and Cammeray. But to my Chinese classmates, the panoramic shots of the Heads and of the harbour foreshores, of Manly ferries pulling into the Quay below towering glass buildings, close-ups of 18-foot skiffs racing across a line of Vaucluse Juniors, and footage of the bridge set against rising cumulus clouds, were altogether a profound revelation. When my classmates turned around and looked at the few Australian students on hand, the expression on their faces indicated that our local standing had risen a notch or two. Australia was a beautiful police state.

Obviously a great deal has changed in China and Australia since the 1970s. We have each followed our own routes to 'open up and reform' (*gaige kaifang*) our domestic societies and economies. Nobody in China considers Australia a police state any more. From reading and conversation, I can reliably report that those early impressions of Sydney Harbour are still in place. After the 2000 Olympics more people than ever are persuaded that Australia is one of the most beautiful and blessed countries on Earth. In the absence of reliable survey data, I would speculate that the most widespread and overriding impression of Australia is of a beautiful, clean and sparsely populated country.

Still, there are a number of stubborn continuities and disturbing discontinuities in contemporary Chinese impressions of Australia. In the past five or six years I have mixed and mingled on many occasions with Australasian experts in China's universities, academies and think-tanks. From them I have learned of two relatively new claims added to one of the old and dated ones in the past decade. First, Pauline Hanson created a widespread and abiding impression that Australians are anxious about Asia and unwelcoming to Chinese people. The view that Australians are fundamentally racist is widespread in élite circles today, spawned by news of Hansonism, reinforced by developments in refugee policy and generally understood in light of the White Australia legacy. Secondly, people are under the impression that Australia is part of Britain, or at least that our national sovereignty is somehow alienated to London. This was brought to attention by the failed referendum on the republic. Third, although they no longer consider Australia a police state, people are still largely persuaded that Australia is a lackey of the US.

These three impressions are not the result of an information black-out or false reporting. In China today, people have access to international cable television and to the World Wide Web, and with, at most, two degrees of separation can claim to know someone who has seen Australia with their own eyes. Contemporary Chinese impressions are for the most part considered judgments, based on acquired knowledge and filtered through powerful Chinese sentiments of national independence and ethnic pride.

In conversation, these three points, touching on sovereignty, independence and racism, are often folded into one question, 'When will Australia grow up?' Doubtless this question reveals as much about prevailing Chinese notions of sovereignty and independence as it does about Australia's alleged lack of them. A country willing to lay out hundreds of millions of dollars at short notice to keep out a few thousand illegal entrants surely takes national sovereignty very seriously indeed. But, I have been asked, why should Australia choose to make a point of national sovereignty on a matter like immigration, and decline to take a stand on the British Queen, or trail unquestioningly in the wake of US foreign policy? I am not lost for answers to this question, nor do I think Australia has much to learn from China on questions of popular sovereignty or the rule of law. But native sovereignty and independence are so highly valued in China that any attempt at an explanation for the unique Australian notion of sovereignty only illustrates the differences that divide us.

Indifference

Over the years I have tried to address these issues, one by one, in the belief that what opinion-makers and others in China happen to think about Australia matters in some material sense to the health of our bilateral relations. But something has changed in Australia's relations with China in the past six or seven years. There is a growing indifference on the part of Australia's governing élite to what people in China or Asia more generally think about Australia. A number of alarming remarks have been attributed to Prime Minister Howard himself, including one that Australia was America's 'deputy' in the region, and another that he would not hesitate to sanction a pre-emptive strike against enemies on foreign soil. His supporters claimed his comments had been read out of context. His critics said he was pandering to a domestic constituency without regard to the impact of his remarks in the region.[5] Both underestimated the Prime Minister's indifference.

John Howard is neither ignorant of the impact his comments have in the region nor blind to their consequences. He appears determined to send out a clear and consistent message to people from the eastern islands of Indonesia to the western states of India. This, at least, is what my Chinese friends and colleagues tell me. The Australian Prime Minister is not merely pandering to a domestic constituency but sending a clear and unequivocal message in the name of Australia to a wider audience of countries in the region. The message goes something like this: we don't *care* what you think about us. We are who we are. Who we are is who we always have been and always will be. We don't propose to change or compromise any of our national values or beliefs simply to accommodate the views or feelings of our Asian neighbours. Australians say it like it is because sincerity is one of the things that makes us Australians. So, too, is toughness in adversity. Take it or leave it — we are not going to be messed around with. And we have big and powerful friends who will come to our aid if anyone steps out of line.

This message may be dispiriting to those Australians who are inclined to defend their country from charges of indifference to the region, or of pandering to great power politics, or indeed of implicit racism. We should rest assured that it is far less disappointing to our neighbours. It recalls a style of Australian behaviour familiar to any ageing regional president or prime minister. It is only the younger generation in China, Japan and South-East Asia that appears at all surprised. For all but the final quarter of the 20th century, Australia did its best to lock out, to patronise and, where possible, to intimidate the people and states of Asia by pointing to powerful allies who would come to our defence if they stepped out of line. The 25-year period from 1972 to 1996 was a historical aberration for our neighbours no less than for ourselves. From this perspective, Australia's effort to become better acquainted with the people, languages and cultures of Asia from the mid-1970s to the mid-1990s was a masquerade that, in John Carroll's phrase, 'fools nobody'.[6] We are what we are, as we always have been, and as far as the current governing élite is concerned, what we always will be. 'We' have little interest in Asia, apart from a hard-edged interest in security and trade. The rest is a matter of indifference.

Historical precedents

Current indifference to Asian views of Australia invites historical reflection on foreign policy precedents in Australia's relations with Asia. How well did an avowedly 'pragmatic' policy of studied indifference to Asian views of Australia serve this country in the first half of the 20th century? What does its revival reveal about Australian notions of national sovereignty today?

The cult of indifference to what people in Asia think about Australia is largely unprecedented in the post-war period. The three decades of effort that went into positioning Australia as a relatively enlightened society with an independent foreign policy has not only been abandoned in the past six or seven years, but abandoned with relish. A conservative backlash against the Australian Enlightenment of the 1970s was perhaps overdue. There were mutterings all along from people currently associated with the Howard Cabinet. Less easily anticipated has been the abandonment of the liberal-conservative ideal of mutual understanding among neighbours that formed the basic post-war consensus on Australia's foreign relations in the region. The ideal of mutual understanding among neighbours has a respectable place in conservative foreign policy thinking. Prime Minister Robert Menzies, for example, commended R.G. Casey on his retirement as Minister for External Affairs for having 'done more than any other man to cultivate friendship with our Asian neighbours, and to improve that mutual understanding which is the true foundation of peace'.[7] Prime Minister Howard has broken not only with the Enlightenment of the 1970s but with the Liberal tradition of the 1950s.

It could be argued that we have moved on from the 1950s, or from the 1970s, to the new world order of the 21st century. Australia's disregard for the views of Asian opinion leaders might be welcomed if it reflected a more general trend of indifference to world opinion and growing self-confidence as a sovereign and independent state. The Prime Minister's repeated comments on Australia's standing in the 'world' suggest otherwise. Alternatively, Australian indifference might be welcomed if it represented a step forward in Australian thinking on the limits of national sovereignty in the new world order. The evidence for this is equally slim. If anything, our cultivated indifference to regional opinion represents a return to notions of great power diplomacy and national sovereignty which have their roots in the Federation era and the Great War.

While current policy directions have little in common with the post-war consensus, they resonate with the 'pragmatic' ethos of the era of Prime Minister William Morris Hughes in the 1910s and 1920s. They get their bearings from Gallipoli and Bradman. And they target Australians who advocate closer relations with the states and societies of Asia as betraying Australia's national heritage. The heritage betrayed is a British one, dating back to the era before the Pacific War and the age of European mass migration, to a mythical time when people knew who they were and conducted their lives with the common sense, pragmatism and sobriety appropriate to their Anglo-Saxon ancestry.

In the aftermath of the Great War, Prime Minister Hughes urged Australians to deal with the world 'as it was' and not 'as we would want it to be'.[8] Hughes was impatient with idealists, and especially dismissive of those who held high the Wilsonian principles of mutual respect and the sovereign equality of nations. In this he anticipated current policy directions. Pragmatic pursuit of the national interest was declared Australia's basic policy framework in the Howard Government's first foreign policy White Paper, in the mid-1990s, and was reaffirmed as the guiding principle for the 21st century in the draft of the second White Paper announced in 2002.[9] The latter heaped scorn on those who harboured vain hopes that Australia might strive to achieve 'international good citizenship'. Such an aspiration, in the words of the White Paper document, 'is a trap for ideologues and the naïve'.[10] Hughes would have nodded his assent.

How well did Billy Hughes' pragmatism serve Australia's long-term national interests? Can pragmatism itself be 'a trap for ideologues and the naïve'? Shortly after his return from the post-war conference in Paris, Hughes gave an account of his diplomatic success there. He likened his own achievements in Paris to those of the Anzacs who had preceded him to Europe. 'White Australia is yours,' he announced to the assembled parliamentarians. '[Our] soldiers have achieved the victory, and my colleagues and I have brought that great principle [of White Australia] back to you from the conference, as safe as it was on the day when it was first adopted.'[11] He also spelled out what these victories meant for the exercise of Australian national sovereignty. Australians alone would decide who came into this country, he told the House of Representatives in September 1919, and the people themselves had decided 'that none should enter in, except such as they chose'.[12]

The Great War was fought for King and Country, of course, not merely to decide 'who should enter in', as Hughes put it. At the federal level, however, the war was rapidly turned to the service of immigration restriction under the rubric of 'White Australia'. This was consistent with the federal level of government after Federation. Among settler colonies of the Pacific Rim, only in Australia did national immigration policy come to bear a sentimental association with national sovereignty. White Australia hinted at something more than the sum of the legislative parts of the Immigration Restriction Act. It elevated the mundane practices of customs officials to the level of a sacred duty.

Racial exclusion, John Hirst points out, was not a significant factor in the decisions and processes leading to Federation 20 years earlier.[13] The sequence actually worked the other way. Federation turned out to be such an insipid affair that it invited more inspiring visions to embolden or supplant it at the national level. Donald Horne has suggested that it was the pragmatism of Federation that accounted for the heavy emphasis placed on White Australia as an ideology in the years after Federation. Pragmatism and racism went together. The 'emptiness of "purpose" in the Constitution', Horne suggested, may have given sharp, extra meaning to the idea of 'Australia for the White Man'. In Canada there was a 'White Canada' movement and there was agitation against coloured immigrants in the US. But in neither country was race chauvinism used as the exclusive means of defining the nation, alone giving it public identity and purpose. In Australia it was given this function. This unique emphasis may have been provided by the accident that in 1901 a federation had occurred without proper rhetorical warning: Federation was given retrospective meaning by the Commonwealth's implementation of the White Australia Policy.

Racial exclusion became important after Federation once elected parliamentarians mounted a higher federal stage from which they could pronounce on elevated matters of national purpose beyond the narrow purview of colonial or state perspectives. 'They needed a great self-defining debate: that ritual debate happened to be on immigration policy,' Donald Horne remarked.[14]

As far as national visions went, Federation and the Great War converged at two points not often to be found at the birth of sovereign nations. First, neither had much to say about national independence. Federation was an act of local administrative unification, effectively centralising the states' colonial ties with Britain through the new Commonwealth Government, while Gallipoli showed the price Australians were prepared to pay in blood to maintain their ties with the Empire. Second, both events helped to craft a distinctive form of sovereignty that focused sentimental regard on territorial borders and border control. At Federation, the founding fathers drafted a national covenant that defined national sovereignty as the right to determine who and what does and does not come into the country. Protectionism and, in time, White Australia gave explicit content to this covenant.

In the aftermath of the Great War, Prime Minster Hughes sealed this covenant with the rhetoric of wartime sacrifice and valour.[15] The basic covenant is so deeply embedded in the rituals and rhetoric of Australian public life that it readily survives the abolition of its specific content

(White Australia or trade protection) and continues to incite passionate feelings about Australian sovereignty. To this day, the exercise of national sovereignty in Australia is chiefly associated with the relatively trivial right of determining who, and what, comes into the country. Native sovereignty and national independence count for little alongside an obsession with border control.[16]

This limited notion of sovereignty seems to be an accidental consequence of the global timing of Federation. Late in the 19th century, national borders were hardening around the world after a period of massive population flows and capital transfers from continent to continent in the preceding century. The period that is remembered in Australia as the Federation era is remembered elsewhere as the concluding phase of the Atlantic Century — a century in which capital and merchandise moved as freely as people under relatively relaxed trade and customs controls. This passage in the development of the global economy cooled off from about the turn of the century, with the introduction of passports and immigration controls and, more drastically, with the imposition of trade barriers.[17] The subsequent period of global contraction yielded an ideal of an autarkic national state that could exercise absolute control over its economic, demographic and cultural boundaries.

This was the moment at which the Australian colonies chose to federate — the new Commonwealth of Australia came into being when border control and racial exclusion were in the air. Australia's Federation was profoundly shaped by this historical experience. The deepest fissures to emerge in debates leading up to Federation in 1901 opened up around disputes between free traders and protectionists, and to a modest degree between champions of greater or lesser restrictions on Asian immigration. In either case, debate turned on the issue of who and what should be let in. The question framed and continues to frame Australian conceptions of sovereignty.

Here a distinction is in order. There was nothing uniquely Australian about preoccupations with border control at the close of the 19th century. National legislation aimed at excluding Chinese immigrants was common among settler states on the Pacific Rim, and Australia was neither the first nor the only country to adopt racial immigration restrictions as national policy. In 1882, the US Congress passed the Chinese Exclusion Act to deny Chinese entry into American ports and to deny resident Chinese the right to naturalisation. The US Chinese Exclusion Act was not repealed until 1943.[18] Canada enforced national restrictions for four decades from 1885 through the imposition of a federal poll tax on Chinese applicants for entry. The poll tax had the effect of limiting the Chinese population of Canada to about 40,000 by the early 1920s — a figure of the same order, relative to population, as the Australian Chinese population during the 'White Australia' era. From the 1920s it was even more restrictive.[19]

What was uniquely Australian was the visionary or patriotic dimension of immigration controls, a feature largely missing from the North American experience. Canada did not become Canada or the North American colonies the USA on the back of arguments about preserving racial purity through a discriminatory immigration regime. Australia did. For the same reason, Canada could abandon the slogan 'White Canada' more readily than Australia can caste aside the baggage of 'White Australia'. Although Australia has practised non-discriminatory immigration procedures since the early 1970s, the right to say who can and cannot come into the country remains the core assumption underlying the exercise of national sovereignty. Immigration controls made us what we were, what we are and, in a sense, what we always will be.

Pragmatism, principle and implications for sovereignty
When the war was over, Hughes travelled to Europe to ensure that this ennobled vision of White Australia was understood and appreciated by the delegates who assembled in Paris to determine the fate of the world in the post-war era. There he fought and won a battle to prevent the international adoption of a Racial Equality clause in the preamble to the Charter of the League of Nations. Prime Minister Hughes seized upon the

sacrifices of Gallipoli to promote a federal obsession with border control beyond Australia to the world at large. He sacrificed the principle of racial equality on the altar of pragmatism.

Hughes was a wily and stubborn politician. He spoke the local dialect of Australian nationalism, and proclaimed it loudly and brazenly to the world, in the conviction that this was what good and honest Australian patriots should do. Australian Britons were all the better distinguished from British ones by their impatient disregard for the niceties of élite diplomacy and their blunt reactions to the effete conceits of international conferences and treaties.[20] Hughes' blunt diplomacy was certainly popular at home. He had a special gift for reading the mood of the electorate and for finding words and images to turn fleeting popular sentiment to his own political advantage. At the same time, he saw himself as an honest, sincere and practical man of action, whose duty it was to represent the Australian national interest as honestly as he could, whatever others may have thought of him or his country on this account. While proclaiming himself a pragmatist, working tirelessly for the national interest, Hughes assumed that the national interest meant preserving the British Empire and keeping Australia white. His pragmatism was driven by ideals to an extent that he rarely acknowledged himself.

His 'romantic pragmatism' made Hughes a formidable political opponent.[21] Hughes' local rivals in Sydney, Melbourne, Brisbane and, in time, Canberra learned to respect the political acumen of the 'Little Digger'. So did the British, Americans and Japanese with whom he argued and negotiated over key clauses of the Peace Agreement in Paris after the war. In time, a good number of people and nations learned to live with defeat at the hands of the romantic Australian pragmatist.

For Hughes every question of principle needed to be reduced to a more basic question of what practical benefit it would confer on Australia before it merited serious attention. He had no patience, for example, with the principle of racial equality supported by US President Woodrow Wilson after the war. To concede the principle of racial equality at an international forum would, he believed, have placed Australian sovereignty at risk. Hughes set out openly and deliberately to undermine international efforts to uphold racial equality as a universal principle in the post-war international order so as to preserve the most important ingredient in Australian sovereignty — the right to say who could come in.

Immediately after the war, Hughes went to Paris to discuss the terms of peace and take part in negotiations leading to the creation of the League of Nations. He took a stand on three main issues: German reparations, Australian mandates over former German territories in the Pacific and racial equality. Ever the practical man, Hughes had a bottom line on each issue. He sought massive punitive damages against Germany, bartered for as many colonial possessions as possible for Australia in the Pacific, and, of special note, fought for the deletion of any reference to racial equality in the formal documents issuing from the conference. The terms of peace, Hughes announced shortly before the Peace Conference began, 'must deal with the world and human nature as they are, and not as they would have them be'.[22] He heaped scorn on those who imagined that a just international settlement might achieve a peaceful outcome. For Hughes, open discussion of the dangers of racial equality marked the only practical way forward.

In the spring of 1919, Hughes became embroiled in a crisis involving the Japanese, British and US delegations in Paris, centring on his unwavering commitment to keeping Australia white. Leading members of the Japanese delegation put forward a proposal to insert a racial equality clause into the preamble of the Covenant to the League of Nations.[23] President Wilson was sympathetic, Lloyd George prevaricated, but Billy Hughes was forthright in his opposition. Any statement asserting the principle of the equality of races would have placed in jeopardy the vision of White Australia for which, by Hughes' account, Australia's young men had fought and died in Europe. To undermine President Wilson's principled support for the racial equality clause, Hughes threatened to stir up anti-Wilson sentiment in local constituencies in the US, where race was a sensitive issue in pending elections.[24] His political apprenticeship in Australia had tutored him sufficiently in populist politics to intimidate a US President. In February and March 1919, the Japanese delegation met with members of the British and American delegations to secure their support for the racial equality clause. While others vacillated, Hughes would not budge. As the Japanese delegation reported to the Japanese Foreign Ministry after one meeting with Hughes, 'The fate of our proposal lies in the hands of one man, the Australian Prime Minister.'[25]

In the end, Australian pragmatism won out. Hughes garnered sufficient support at the conference to reduce the vote in favour of inserting a racial equality clause into the preamble to a simple majority. This was enough to scuttle it. For Hughes, the defeat of the racial equality clause was a triumphal demonstration of Australian national sovereignty — specifically, the national right to determine who could and could not come into the country. For Japan, it was a humiliation not forgotten to this day.

Hughes, it should be noted, had no problem acknowledging the equality of races 'out there' in the world. But he would not admit the equality of races 'in here' within the Australian nation itself. Hughes chiefly objected to the racial equality clause on the grounds that the Australian Federal Government alone would say who could and could not come into the country, and he reserved the right to employ race as a category for exclusion. Hughes believed this was a local issue of no particular relevance to others. What others thought was of little consequence. Issues of immigration and race were 'purely domestic matters', he told the Japanese delegation at Versailles. Immigration was none of their business.[26]

Pragmatism and its consequences
In fact, significant international repercussions did flow from the defeat of the racial equality clause in 1919. When Hughes took to badgering British Prime Minister Lloyd George over the clause, the South African representative, General J.C. Smuts, was asked to intervene. Smuts advised the Japanese delegation

that Hughes spoke with an independent voice and not on behalf of Britain. He added, for good effect, that Hughes 'was by nature very narrow-minded and was not the kind of man to consider *international implications*'.[27] Hughes failed to acknowledge the degree to which international diplomacy was shaped by 'domestic matters' or to concede that his single-minded pursuit of Australian domestic issues at the Paris convention could shape international relations for decades to come.

What was the practical outcome of Hughes' 'pragmatic' foreign policy? On these questions our Asian-language sources are variously shrill and silent. They are loud and emphatic in Japan but still largely silent in China. First, his behaviour alienated the Japanese Government at a time when Australia could ill afford to give offence. Major E.L. Piesse, Australia's Director of Military Intelligence, noted at the time that Hughes' attitude caused grave offence in Japan and that memories of this humiliation could have long-term consequences for Australia. Hughes, wrote Piesse, 'has chosen to emphasise the national distinctions between the Japanese and ourselves in a way that could not fail to be offensive to a high spirited people ... their effect in Japan has been most serious'.[28] Hughes may have been indifferent but the offence was neither forgiven nor forgotten. Today, Hughes is far less well remembered in Australia than he is in Japan, where his exploits in Paris continue to be retold, again and again, in popular and textbook histories of Japanese nationalism and Australian racism. The 'Little Digger' is considered to be the quintessential Australian: rude, ignorant of world affairs, narrow-minded and deaf to the demands of international good citizenship.[29]

The second international repercussion was an indirect one, though no less important for the post-war international order than the humiliation of Japan. The American delegates came up with a face-saving gesture to compensate the Japanese delegation for the defeat of the racial equality clause. Sean Brawley mounts a persuasive case that the Americans made a secret concession to the Japanese delegation in the closing days of the convention. To mollify the aggrieved Japanese, they acceded to Japan's request to take control of German possessions in China which Japanese forces had confiscated from Germany during the war. By trading Chinese territory for the principle of racial equality, Brawley writes, 'Wilson had to give Japan "what they should not have" because he could not give them what they *should* have' — an international commitment to the principled equality of races.[30] By his actions, Hughes had ensured that Wilson could not deliver on racial equality.

For China's domestic politics, this secret agreement was one of the most far-reaching decisions ever taken in an international forum. Now it was the turn of the Chinese people to feel humiliated. China's delegation in Paris, representing the new Republican Government, protested, but to no avail. In Beijing the Prime Minister fell, and with him the hopes of the liberal parliamentary movement, which fell in turn to Leninist parties in the wake of the fateful decision at Versailles. Hughes' 'pragmatic' interest in scuttling the racial equality clause at the Paris conference led to the downfall of the new Chinese liberal republic.

It did more. On hearing the news from Paris, students took to the streets of Beijing in May 1919, founding a movement that is still remembered in Chinese communist historiography as the inaugural or founding moment of the communist revolution: the May Fourth Movement. While protesting the surrender of Chinese territories to Japan, students brandished signs calling for the removal of the democratic government of China and an end to all foreign imperialism. Leading public figures in Shanghai, Canton and Beijing emerged to denounce the republican government for failing to defend the country's national sovereignty. Russian agents and representatives of the Communist International moved in among students, teachers, workers and Chinese political reformers, setting up networks of radical cells that would introduce a new and more powerful form of government that would rid China of Japanese, British, American and other foreign imperialists for ever. Within a few years, Sun Yatsen abandoned his commitment to liberal democracy, signed up with the Russians, reorganised his Chinese Nationalist Party into a Leninist party, and set up a single-party state in Canton — the precursor to the Communist Party one. In 1921, the Comintern's small political cells converged to form the Chinese Communist Party. As a party of the working class, the communist movement was of little consequence. Once it learned to harness mass discontent with foreign humiliation and colonial infringements of China's territory, the communist movement grew to become the most powerful political organisation in the country.

We would be drawing a long bow to attribute the birth of communist China to the words and actions of Hughes at Versailles. Still, we can place the actions of Prime Minister Hughes at the peace conference into a clear causal sequence stretching from Paris to Tokyo, and across the Sea of Japan to Beijing, even if these international outcomes were only partly of Hughes' making. By sticking to his narrowly 'pragmatic' defence of Australian sovereignty — conceived as border control — and publicly professing racism on the world stage, Hughes gave succour to China's communists. Australia was one of several sites of anti-Chinese racism on the Pacific Rim. But only the Australian Government adopted a principled and patriotic position on the subject. Publicly enunciated as White Australia, Australia's unique brand of patriotic racism was a source of constant humiliation to people in China and to people of Chinese descent in South-East Asia, in the Americas and in Australia itself. So it remains to this day. Humiliation is a powerful instrument of nationalist politics. The communists used it well to secure victory in 1949 and to win international acceptance among Chinese communities the world over for decades to come.

Conclusion
Chinese impressions of Australian public life today invite us to reflect on the relationship between our hard-headed pragmatism and our limited ideal of national sovereignty. We could, of course, reject these impressions out of hand as biased or ill-

informed. The alternative is to take them seriously if only for pragmatic reasons. They give us occasion to reflect historically on the link between our avowed pragmatism and the implicit idealism that underpins it, grounded in Australia's case in a particular historical vision of national sovereignty. In Australia, a recurring obsession with border control overshadows aspects of national sovereignty which other states take seriously. To turn this observation around, Australia's institutional indifference to native sovereignty and to national independence leaves patriotic sentiment nowhere to go but out on patrol.

When pragmatism is elevated to a principle it, too, can become 'a trap for ideologues and the naïve', no less than unreflective idealism.[31] There is little to be said for idealistic future-watching divorced from achievable outcomes. That said, it is not only idealists who fashion futures. When Hughes dealt with the world 'as it was' he helped make the world what it would yet become. He was rightly wary of Japan's potential for overseas expansion and China's capacity to 'wake up and shake the world', but his romantic pragmatism did little to deter them. In the 1920s, Australia's leading role in undermining the principle of racial equality and its practice of racial exclusion in the name of national sovereignty significantly diminished the prospects for a just international settlement in the post-war era. Naïve pragmatism was, in the end, a cause of war and revolution, not a means of avoiding them. Australian pragmatism yielded the very spectre which pragmatists most deeply feared: the emergence of powerful and heavily armed states in East Asia.

Today, contemporary Australian foreign policy seems paradoxical to observers in China. While Australia closely follows the US lead, in pursuit of avowedly pragmatic goals, it is actually helping to remake the world according to an American vision of how the world 'should be'. In November 2002, the Bush administration rejected out of hand European pleas for Washington to deal with the world 'as it is' in dealing with Iraq. The *Washington Post*'s Jim Hoagland rose to defend the Bush administration. The Europeans' appeal to deal with the world 'as it is', he pointed out, 'ignores how rapidly and dramatically the world is changing ... Equivocation and tinkering — the heart and soul of Europe's current diplomacy — is rapidly falling behind history's ever accelerating curve'.[32] In fact, Washington seeks to 'straighten out the untidy world in which we live', another observer argues, without reference to alliances, multilateral frameworks, rules or even treaties.[33] On the one side is a vision of a rules-based international system, founded on the dignity and equality of sovereign nations and, on the other, a vision of the US as a world system in which national sovereignty plays little part. A country such as Australia, which places little value on native sovereignty and national independence, may not appreciate the difference between a rules-based and a Washington-based system. Other countries in the region do appreciate the difference, and they evaluate us on the same account.

To the outside observer, Australia's foreign policy does not appear to lack vision or ideology; it merely lacks Australian vision or ideology. This paradox is at once a measure of our dependence and the stamp of our autonomy. Our dependence on the US provides an autonomous space within which Australia can be merely 'pragmatic', a luxury Washington has long since discarded and which President George W. Bush can ill afford.

We might well reflect on the lasting significance of a characteristic Australian notion of national sovereignty that would focus on the sovereign right to determine who does and does not come into the country to the exclusion of native sovereignty or international independence. No matter how we may try to deny or to escape the racist implications of this form of sovereignty — for example, by pointing to the non-discriminatory nature of our current immigration and refugee policies — we cannot avoid returning to the source of the distinctive conception of sovereignty itself. The right to say who can come in to this country is the foundational assumption of the Australian nation. It made us who we were, who we are and who we always will be. That said, we cannot escape the origins of this skewed conception of sovereignty in the White Australia Policy. We can certainly evacuate our conception of sovereignty of its racist content but we can no more deny its origins in racism than American historians can deny that Thomas Jefferson kept slaves.

Australian racism will continue to surface in Australia's relations with the region, in Australian nationalism and as a dominant theme in Australian history, not because nationalists are all 'racist' nor because historians all don black arm-bands. It will surface for the same reason that slavery surfaces in celebrations of American patriotism or in reflections on US history. The more Americans dwell on their sovereign right to be counted free and equal, the more they discover the inequality and bondage that has at times characterised their nation. The more Australians stress our sovereign right to patrol our borders — by advertising that we alone determine who comes into this country — the more we focus the region's attention on why we feel so keenly about it. However assiduously we may cultivate indifference to the views of our neighbours, this is one impression of theirs that is unlikely to fade away.

Footnotes

1. Sydney Airport, 12 April, 1966: Reporter: 'What are your impressions of Australia?' Dylan: 'Australia isn't a very nice place for lots of people — people like Orientals and Negroes.' Reporter: 'Perhaps you'd better be careful what you say.' Melbourne Airport, 17 April, 1966: Reporter: 'What do you think about Australia?' Dylan: 'Since I was a little boy I have heard about Australia. I once knew someone who knew somebody who knew somebody whose grandfather was supposed to have been to Australia. This gave me a tremendous curiosity to find out whether this fellow really did have a grandfather.' From Hamilton, Paul and Karen Morden. *The Freespieling Bob Dylan*. www.idler.co.uk/html/frontsection/dylan.htm

2. PM signals more action for troops. *The Age*, 2 July, 2003. Mr Howard made a similar claim in April 2002. See Transcript of the Prime Minister the Hon John Howard MP. The Prime Minister's Closing Address, Liberal Party 49th Federal Council, Hyatt Hotel, Canberra. 14 April, 2002. http://www.pm.gov.au/news/speeches/2002/speech 1596.htm. I wish to thank Meg Gurry for the 2002 reference.

3. See the Pew Research Center web site at www.people-press.org

4. John Carroll, for example, argues that the countries of Asia envy our close alliance with the US, applaud our pragmatic foreign policy and respect the values and institutions which distinguish Australia from other countries in the region. 'It is John Howard,' Carroll writes, 'not Paul Keating, who has got these relationships right.' See Carroll, John. 2003. Howard navigating a safe diplomatic course. *Australian Financial Review*, 9 January, 2003.

5. Michelle Grattan observes that John Howard's comments and responses seem to have been made with an eye to his 'domestic constituency'. *The Age*, 4 December, 2002.

6. Carroll, John. 2003. Howard navigating a safe diplomatic course. *Australian Financial Review*, 9 January, 2003.

7. *The Age*, 25 January, 1960. Cited in Millar, T.B. (ed.). 1972. *Australian Foreign Minister: The Diaries of R.G. Casey 1951–1960*. p.12. London: Collins. I wish to thank Antonia Finnane for this reference.

8. Cited in Meaney, Neville. 1976. *The Search for Security in the Pacific, 1901–1914*. p.45. Sydney: Sydney University Press.

9. The White Paper that framed foreign and trade policy in the first two terms of the Howard Government was titled *In The National Interest* (August 1997).

10 Foreign Minister Alexander Downer. Advancing the National Interest: Australia's Foreign Policy Challenge. National Press Club, Canberra. 7 May, 2002.
11 Hughes to Parliament. Reported in Deane, P.E. *Australia's Rights: The Fight at the Peace Table*. See ABC web site.
12 Cited in Hudson, W.J. 1978. *Billy Hughes in Paris: The Birth of Australian Diplomacy*. p.66. Melbourne: Thomas Nelson.
13 Hirst, John. Chinese Immigration and Australian Sentiment at Federation. In Couchman, Sophie, John Fitzgerald and Paul Macgregor (eds), forthcoming, *After the Rush: Regulation, Participation and Australia's Chinese Communities, 1860-1940*.
14 Horne, Donald. 2000. *Billy Hughes: Prime Minister of Australia 1915-1923*. pp.75–6. Melbourne: Black Ink.
15 'White Australia,' Hughes confided in a memo at the Paris Peace Conference,' is the cornerstone of the national edifice.' Fitzhardinge, L.F. 1979. *The Little Digger: William Morris Hughes, A Political Biography, Volume II, 1914–1952*. p.398. Sydney: Angus & Robertson. His Private Secretary, Percy Deane, later recalled of Hughes' work at the Paris conference that 'the Prime Minister was called upon to battle desperately for this [White Australia], compared to which our sacrifices in war, our achievements, our gains, fade into insignificance. For we would gladly sacrifice as much again — or give up all that we have gained – rather than forsake this policy.' Deane, P.E. 1920. *Australia's Rights: The Fight at the Peace Table*. Political Pamphlet. This reference can be found on the ABC Federation web site http://www.abc.net.au/federation/fedstory/ep2/ep2_places.htm. C.E.W. Bean, the historian who gave shape to the Anzac legend, was persuaded that Australians had fought and died at Gallipoli for the one social ideal they knew, 'that of race'. See Meaney, Neville. 1999. *Towards a New Vision: Australia and Japan — Through A Hundred Years*. p.25. East Roseville, NSW: Kangaroo Press.
16 See, for example, the exhibition mounted by Australian Customs to commemorate the Centenary of Federation, which equates people with fruit and worm-eaten wood. The opening exhibits feature confiscated ivory, woodwork and narcotics. Later exhibits culminate in a display of sandals and Thermos flasks from the hopeful Chinese refugees who stepped on to Australian beaches in the 1990s.
17 O'Rourke, Kevin and Jeffrey Williamson. 1999. *Globalisation and History: The Evolution of a Nineteenth Century Atlantic Economy*. Boston, Mass.: MIT Press.

18 Even after repeal of the Act in 1943, the level of immigration from China was formally restricted to about 100 people a year until Congress passed the non-discriminatory Immigration Act of 1965. Gyory, Andrew. 1998. *Closing the Gate: Race, Politics, and the Chinese Exclusion Act*. Chapel Hill, NC: University of North Carolina Press. Pan, Lynn (ed.). 1999. *The Encyclopedia of the Chinese Overseas*. pp.261–73. Cambridge, Mass.: Harvard University Press.

19 From 1923, the Canadian Government enforced an even stricter regime. The 1923 Exclusion Act was so rigorously enforced that it is reported to have limited the entry of Chinese settlers into Canada to a total of about two dozen people up to the end of World War II at a rate of about one person a year. Far more Chinese entered Australia in the same period. The Canadian restrictions were eased in 1947 to allow entry of close family relatives of Canadian Chinese citizens. Still, independent Chinese immigrants were not granted entry until 1962. Chinese Canadians were also subject to discriminatory legislation that was in some respects similar to Australian legislation and in others more severe. In British Columbia, for example, Chinese Canadians were disenfranchised in provincial and federal elections from 1875 to 1947. Pan, Lynn (ed.). 1999. *The Encyclopedia of the Chinese Overseas*. pp.234–47. Cambridge, Mass.: Harvard University Press.

20 See Horne, *Billy Hughes*, pp.109–13 and *passim*.

21 Donald Horne applies the term 'romantic pragmatist' to Hughes. Ibid.

22 Fitzhardinge, L.F. 1979. *The Little Digger Vol. II, 1914–1952*. p.372.

23 Two drafts were proposed, one of which was further modified before the clause was put to a vote. The first draft, preferred by the Japanese delegation, read: 'The equality of nations being a basic principle of the League, the High Contracting Parties agree that concerning the treatment and rights to be accorded to aliens in their territories they will not discriminate, either in law or in fact, against any person or persons on account of his or their race or nationality.' The alternative version read: 'The equality of nations being a basic principle of the League of Nations, the High Contracting Parties agree that concerning the treatment of aliens in their territories, they will accord them, as far as it lies in their legitimate powers, equal treatment and rights, in law and in fact, without making any distinction on account of their race or nationality.' Ibid., p.401.

24 Brown, Frank C. n.d. *They Called Him Billy.* p.155. Sydney: Peter Huston. Brown notes approvingly, 'The fact that the United States President was a politician with a politician's weaknesses, had been overlooked by almost everybody at the Peace Conference. But not by Billy.'
25 Cited in Fitzhardinge, *The Little Digger Vol. II.* p.405.
26 Ibid., p.407–10.
27 Ibid., p.404.
28 Major Piesse, March 24, 1919, Naval Office, Melbourne. MP, NAA 1049/1, 1918/049. See ABC web site.
29 That Hughes was seen in Japan as the 'typical Australian' was made clear to Australian delegates to the Institute of Pacific Relations as early as the 1920s. See Brawley, Sean. 1997. *The White Peril: Foreign Relations and Asian Immigration to Australasia and North America, 1919–1978.* p.97. Kensington: University of NSW Press.
30 Brawley, *The White Peril*, Chapter 4, *passim*, esp. p.33. See also Hudson, *Billy Hughes in Paris*, p.58.
31 Foreign Minister Alexander Downer. Advancing the National Interest: Australia's Foreign Policy Challenge. National Press Club, Canberra. 7 May, 2002.
32 *International Herald Tribune*, 18 November, 2002.
33 Lewis, Anthony. 2002. Bush and Iraq. pp.4–6. *New York Review of Books*, 7 November, 2002.

2. 'BEFORE WE CAME TO THIS COUNTRY, WE HEARD THAT ENGLISH LAWS WERE GOOD AND KIND TO EVERYBODY'

CHINESE IMMIGRANTS' VIEWS OF COLONIAL AUSTRALIA

Paul Macgregor

> *The practice of offering gratuitous impertinence or insult to persons of other nationality now and again meets with an unexpected check ... and the following is very illustrative of the fact: 'A young gentleman — I suppose we must so term him — was a few evenings since riding in a Fitzroy cab, having for a fellow passenger a respectable looking Chinaman, and flippantly remarked, "John, you sabbee, ride in a cabbee." He was somewhat disconcerted by an intimation from the "Chinee" that if he (the gentlemanly European) wanted to converse with him, he, the "Chinee" would "be happy to accommodate him in English, French, Italian or Chinese, but he must decline a conversation in broken English or slang" ... The particular "John" whose privacy had been intruded upon was Mr Kong Meng, the Chinese merchant, whose lingual accomplishments are well known.'*[1]

When asked to present a paper based on the material gathered for the Asian Accounts of Australia Project, I noted that there was nothing in Chinese about Australia noted from the National Library of Australia collection that dates from the 19th century. I wondered if there was some connection between this and the multilingual accomplishments of Lowe Kong Meng, who was perhaps the pre-eminent Chinese merchant and community leader in Australia from 1853 until his death in 1888.

I reflected on what documents I knew of that otherwise exist in Australia's public record from this period. My immediate reaction was that there are few known records in the public domain in Australia dating prior to the 1890s that present a Chinese perspective on the nature of Australia; less still of this is written in Chinese text.

Is this purely a function of the small size of the Chinese-speaking population at this time? From a couple of thousand in 1851, the numbers of Chinese in Australia quickly rose to about 50,000 in the Victorian goldrush[2] in the 1850s and, while the concentrations of settlement moved from colony to colony in the next four decades, the total population of Chinese throughout Australia seems to have fluctuated between 30,000 and 40,000 until the early 20th century,[3] and then slowly diminished to 12,000 by the 1940s.[4]

There were at least two short-lived Chinese-language newspapers published in Victoria in the 1850s and 1860s. The first that is known about is *The English and Chinese Advertiser*, published in Ballarat from 1856. Six issues only of this weekly broadsheet are known to have survived. It was mainly — as the name implies — literally a publication of advertisements, as well as government notices to the Chinese from colonial officials. It was published by an Englishmen, Robert Bell, and possibly survived only for two years.[5] Another attempt, with a foolscap-sized newspaper in Melbourne, and also published by an Englishman (E. Whitehead), was the *Fi-pao*, translated as *Flying Intelligencer*. No copies of this remain extant, but the first issue is described in an article in *The Argus* in October 1868.[6]

It was not until the 1890s that we have the first development of a Chinese-language newspaper which included substantial articles. This was the *Chinese Australian Herald*,[7] which was followed a few years later by the *Tung Wah News/Times*.[8] From then until the 1940s, a range of Chinese Australian newspapers flourished.[9] Substantial holdings of these newspapers are held in the Mitchell Library in Sydney and the State Library of Victoria, and one of the tasks of the Chinese Heritage of Australian Federation Project (CHAF) has been to create an online index of the *Tung Wah News/Times*. The CHAF Project is a collaboration jointly initiated by Professor John Fitzgerald at La Trobe University and myself, funded primarily through the Australia Foundation, the National Council for the Centenary of Federation and the Australian Research Council. Further information about this project and its outcomes can be found at the project's web site at www.chaf.lib.latrobe.edu.au

It is a curious question as to why it took 40 years for Chinese-language newspapers to take root in Australia, and to then flourish while at the same time the potential readership was decreasing. This may, of course, relate to the wider issue of when the Western concept of the newspaper began to be adopted in Chinese societies, either in China or in the diaspora.[10] It may also have to do with the improvements in technologies of communication and transportation after the 1880s, which may have reduced the costs of printing and enabled broader distribution beyond a local audience (Melbourne and Sydney newspapers are known to have been distributed around Australia, and to New Zealand and the Pacific). It may also be because of the increasing interest among the Australian Chinese communities in keeping abreast of the major political and social changes in China which accelerated in the last years of the Qing Dynasty and into the Republican period.

But the lack of Chinese-language newspapers from the 1850s to the 1880s may also relate to the attitudes in this period of Chinese Australian community leaders, and perhaps especially the merchants with the money to invest in establishing a newspaper venture. I will return to the role of the merchants.

First, I would like to consider other ways of finding Chinese voices in Australia dating from the 1850s to the 1880s.

Private or business papers and correspondence of Chinese in Australia, written in Chinese, are rare items from this period (although some may still lurk in the homes of descendents of early Chinese pioneers). The earliest substantial first-person document is the journal of Jong Ah Sing (Jong Ah Sing?), a Chinese miner incarcerated in a lunatic asylum in Victoria for the last 33 years of his life from the 1860s onwards. This diary, written in a unique and difficult style of English influenced by Chinese syntax, has been reviewed by Yuan Fang Shen in her *Dragon Seed in the Antipodes*,[11] and also has been translated and published in full by Ruth Moore and John Tully.[12] The earliest substantial business records in Australia are those of the Foon Kee Company of Little Bourke Street in Melbourne, which date to about 1905, and are held in our museum.[13]

The earliest known Chinese book about Australia is a Chinese-English phrase book, of unspecified date and place of publication, also in our museum's collection.[14] It provides handy phrases in English, along with Chinese translations and other lines of Chinese characters, which, when pronounced in either of two Cantonese dialects, approximate the sound of the English word. The book also provides lists of place names on the Californian and Victorian goldfields, again with translations and phonetic equivalents. Occasionally the author provides some short commentary about a location, such as saying that 'Emerald Hill is beside the sea, diagonally opposite Melbourne city. That's where the See Yup Company is located'. At another point he notes that he 'lived in the town of Castlemaine for many years, and so is able to provide more names for goldfields in that district'. Something of the lifestyle and concerns of a Chinese colonist can be ascertained from the types of phrases provided: mining gold, dealing with court cases, buying goods, trading, talking with English women, cooking, seeing a doctor, returning to China and the like. Yet the absence of growing or trading in vegetables probably locates this book in the 1860s, before the increase in market gardening as a major activity in the 1870s.[15]

A similar book was discovered in Hong Kong in recent decades, which appears to be published in the 1880s and is specific in content to Sydney. This was analysed by James Hayes at a conference at our museum in 1993.[16]

It would seem, though, that in order to find the majority of Chinese accounts of Australia in this period, it is necessary to rely on English-language texts written by Chinese or written by Europeans who are recounting the words and views of Chinese.

There is a perhaps surprising number of these sources, in a variety of contexts. We have letters to the English-language newspapers, petitions to parliament,[17] letters of protest to the Government, memorials and testimonials to British and colonial dignatories. A number of parliamentary and other government inquiries recorded the words of Chinese witnesses. Court cases also record the views of Chinese involved in litigation or charged with criminal offences. Christian missions to the Chinese in colonial Australia included Chinese immigrants as evangelists, deacons and ministers — and the views of these men are included in church correspondence and publications.

The pages of metropolitan and country newspapers are rich sources of information about Chinese people and their views, and they have only recently begun to be systematically analysed for information about and by Chinese Australians. The Chinese references in newspapers in two particular provincial Victorian towns have recently been made available to the public. An index to Chinese references in the *Bendigo Advertiser* has been made available through a joint project between the Golden Dragon Museum in Bendigo and La Trobe University.[18] Articles about Chinese in the newspapers of the Beechworth district have been extracted and compiled into a book by independent researcher Vivienne McWaters.[19]

A more tangential 'account' of Australia is the analysis of photographs and other images of and by Chinese. What and who are being photographed? For what purpose, and for what audience? To enable a more sophisticated analysis of visual records as documents of Chinese Australian history, a new research collaboration has begun between our Chinese Museum, La Trobe University and the Australian Science and Technology Heritage Centre. This is being funded through the Australian Research Council, with PhD candidate Sophie Couchman creating an online annotated catalogue of images of Chinese and their descendants in Australasia, China and South-East Asia.[20]

What accounts of Australia do these sources, produced by Chinese in Australia, give? In considering this question, I was required to examine, as I increasingly do in my role at the Chinese Museum, what is the nature of Australia and the nature of Australian culture. In the context of this Asian Accounts Project, are 'Chinese' outsiders to 'Australia' commenting from a cultural as well as a geographical distance, or are they part of the developing Australian culture? Are accounts of Chinese community life in Australia accounts of Australia? Has this project fed inadvertently into the 'us and them' mentality by focusing on articles which place a cultural and/or geographical distance between 'Asians' and 'Australians'?

When looking for documents relevant to my paper, I reviewed the reports by Cheong Cheok Hong of his tour of inspection of Chinese mission districts in rural Australia in 1887[21] and William Young's report on the Chinese population of Victoria in 1868.[22] Both notably talk only about the Chinese quarters, camps and communities which they visited. My initial reaction was — well, they're only talking about Chinese, not about Australian society in general. So I, at first, discounted these documents for this paper. But then we had the Chinese New Year Festival recently in Melbourne, with a grand new dragon just arrived from Foshan in Guangdong parading through the streets of Melbourne and, of course, the ubiquitous lions and firecrackers, and tens of thousands of Chinese Melbournians thronging with the rest of the community. Afterwards, a non-Chinese friend of mine commented, 'It was great — it was just like being in Hong Kong.' My immediate reaction was — no, it's just like being in Melbourne, where Chinese parades have been around for longer than Australian Rules Football, and where the Chinese dragon has been a centrepiece of the Moomba Parade since 1953, and where Europeans and Chinese have been enjoying Chinese festivities together since at least the 1860s.

So, I thought, we keep separating our accounts of Chinese Australian life from accounts of Australian life in general. And I asked myself, should I maintain this separation when framing this paper?

In the end, this led me to critically focus on the views of three key 'spokespeople' of the Chinese community in mid-colonial Victoria: the 'merchants', Louis Ah Mouy and Lowe Kong Meng, and the 'evangelist', Cheong Cheok Hong. These three appear quite frequently in the records of the day and are commonly referred to in histories of the Chinese in colonial Victoria. None of these men has yet received the critical biographical examination that their roles warrant. Oddie gives a cursory account of the 'merchant élite' in the colonial Chinese community, and goes little beyond the comment that the merchants were few and were leaders, and that the majority were labourers. Kong Meng and Ah Mouy get a few hundred words; Cheong is only 'a Chinese missionary'.[23] Kathryn Cronin gives somewhat more biographical details about each of these three, yet her book is mainly an examination of British Australian attitudes to the Chinese in their midst, and provides little in the way of an account of the development of the Chinese community and economic activity.[24]

Contrary to the stereotype of the Chinese as a temporary sojourner in Australian colonial life, these three men committed themselves to lifelong settlement in the rapidly developing post-goldrush Victoria, and set about taking active roles in contributing to the creation of what Victorian colonial life would become.

What do these men offer us about their attitude to life in Australia in the 1850s to the 1880s?

The key text I will consider is *The Chinese Question in Australia*, published in Melbourne in 1879, in response to the campaign to keep Chinese sailors from working on Australian coastal shipping routes.[25] Nominally the work of Kong Meng, Ah Mouy and Cheong, it is probable that the main writer was Cheong. The tone and style is commensurate with that of the extensive Cheong correspondence archives held at the National Library and our Chinese Museum. Kong Meng and Ah Mouy would have lent their considerable renown in colonial life to increase the repute of the pamphlet. Kong Meng was a prolific writer of letters to the Government regarding injustices to the Chinese, so he would also have made a contribution to the content.[26] By 1879, each of these two merchants was a prominent entrepreneur, active in the highest reaches of colonial society, about 50 years of age, living in grand houses in Malvern and Middle Park. Cheong, by contrast, having arrived in 1863 as a 12-year-old, was only 27 in the year the pamphlet was written.[27] Educated in Melbourne to matriculation, he had a flair for English rhetoric and was well versed in the philosophies, histories and politics of Britain and China, in particular, and international affairs in general.

In broad terms, the pamphlet argues that the West forced China to open itself to the international community, to welcome the benefits of Western civilisation and to sign treaties permitting the free flow of foreigners into China, and Chinese into the territories of the Western signatory nations. Yet in the Australian part of the British Empire, there was a move to exclude and discriminate against Chinese. Much of the pamphlet argues that the terms of the treaty justify equality of treatment for all people as a moral principle. Pointing out the hypocrisy in the views of the Western nations, it demonstrates that discrimination and attacks against Westerners in China would invite the gunboats to bear down on China, yet the same treatment against Chinese in Australia goes unpunished. The pamphlet's arguments are placed in an international context, with various examples of Western countries' living conditions, political views, citizens and philosophies compared favourably and unfavourably with those of China.

In this broader context, arguing the specifics of these issues in Australia affords us some ideas of how Australia was viewed by Cheong, Ah Mouy and Kong Meng.

According to the pamphlet, Australia is a place which is vast, under-populated and ripe for response to the efforts of labouring immigrants from around the world. By opening China up to the nations of Western Europe, Cheong et al. say that 'we [Chinese] learned that there were vast portions of the earth's surface which were almost destitute of inhabitants, and which were capable of supporting the redundant millions of Europe and Asia'.[28] Australia at the beginning of the goldrush 'was a great continent nearly half as large again as China, and containing only a few hundreds of thousands of civilised people thinly scattered around the coast ... rich in the precious metals and very fertile'. Now, they argue 25 years later, China 'is estimated to contain not much less than 2,000,000 square miles of territory, and 400,000,000 people. Australia comprises an area of close upon 3,000,000 square miles, and it contains no more than 2,100,000 white people, and a few thousand black. In our own land, millions of men, women, and children — yes, millions — think of the horror and pity of it! — have died of starvation during the last year'.

'Would you seek to debar us,' they go on to say, 'from participating in the abundance with which a bountiful Providence — or, as our Master Confucius says, the most great and sovereign God — rewards the industrious and the prudent in this country? Did man create it, or did God? And if it be His work, then can it be disputed that it is open to all who cannot obtain the means of subsistence in their own country, and who will faithfully conform to the laws of this?'

Australia is also clearly seen by the authors as being predominantly an English country, and clearly a part of the British Empire, with all the privileges and responsibilities this implies. Yet it is also a locus of the benefits of an international borderless community created through multilateral treaties permitting the free flow of immigrants between nations. Australia is, in theory, governed by English principles of fairness, which are also congruent with Christian values, and, moreover, at heart are similar to Confucian precepts. When the Western powers argued for China's engagement with the world, say the authors, the argument was that 'God hath made of one blood all nations of men, for to dwell on all the face of the earth. We are all his children. Let us draw together the ties of commercial amity, and live and do business together like friends and brethren'. As a consequence, the Chinese, they say, 'felt sure that such an enlightened people as the English ... would eagerly welcome the arrival of some thousands of frugal, laborious, patient, docile and persevering immigrants'.

The writers add that the English were 'a great, free people ... which owes so much of the prosperity of its mother country to the fact that it has been, for many centuries past, the refuge and the asylum of foreigners flying from religious persecution and political oppression in their own countries. In this way, its woollen, crêpe, and silk manufactures were established by fugitives from the Netherlands and from France; and thus its hospitality to strangers has been twice blessed. It blessed those whom it welcomed to its shores, and it blessed its own industries by the arts and processes which these aliens communicated to their hosts. And if an island so small as the United Kingdom made no demur about opening its arms to all comers, and was not afraid of the competition of these exiles, but greeted them as fellow-workers, surely there is room enough in this large continent [of Australia]'.

They continue, 'Your missionaries came among us, and read from your Scriptures beautiful precepts like those of Confucius and Mencius. They spoke to us of the brotherhood of man, and told us that the foundation principle of the social religion of Englishmen was this — "Ye shall do unto others as ye would they should do unto you". And this, also, is the sentiment of our own Great Teacher'.

Australia was also a country which had undeniably profited from the skills and enterprise of Chinese immigrants. 'It cannot be denied that our countrymen have been good colonists. Had it not been for them, the cultivation of vegetables, so indispensable to the maintenance of health in a hot climate like this, would scarcely have been attempted in the neighbourhood of some of the goldfields; and the mortality of children would have been very much greater than it really has been. Lease or sell half an acre of apparently worthless land to a small party of Chinamen, and, if there is access to any kind of water or manure, they will transform it, by their system of intensive husbandry, into a most prolific garden, and will make it yield such a rapid succession of crops as will excite the astonishment and admiration of European market-gardeners. As fishermen and itinerant fishmongers, our countrymen have been equally serviceable to the community; and as hawkers of all kinds of useful wares, they are indefatigable, cheerful, obliging, and patient'.

Yet the authors express amazement at the amount of prejudice, discrimination and abuse meted out to the Chinese in Australia: 'Nothing, we submit, can be more unreasonable, unjust, or undeserved, than the clamour which has been raised against the Chinese by a portion of the people of this colony; for we refuse to believe that that clamour expresses the opinions and feelings of the great bulk of the community'. Nevertheless, they see that such prejudice does not extend to non-British Europeans. 'You do not endeavour to exclude Germans, or Frenchmen, or Italians, or Danes, or Swedes. There are men of all these nationalities here'.

On the key issue of a supposed downward effect on wages of European workmen if Chinese labour is allowed free rein in Australia, the authors argue this to be a sentimental rather than real grievance. They state that 'the earnings of the Chinese labourer in his native land are quite inconsiderable by comparison with the rate of wages current in Australia, is undeniable. But human nature is human nature all the world over; and the Chinaman is just as fond of money, and just as eager to earn as much as he can, as the most grasping of his competitors. There are Irishmen in this colony who have known what it was to work for four or five shillings a week in the island they came from; but when they emigrate to Victoria, they are not content to put up with lesser wages than they find other farm hands earning'.

'And so it will be,' they continue, 'after a very little time, with our own countrymen here. Living among people who have invented thousands of artificial wants, and thousands of means of gratifying them, the expenditure of the Asiatic will soon rise to the European level, because his habits and his mode of living will approximate to those of his neighbours; and, as it is, it cannot have escaped the observation of persons who have been brought much into contact with the Chinese in Victoria, that the diet of such of them as are tolerably prosperous becomes more generous and costly in proportion to the improvement of their circumstances, and that those who marry and settle here conform to British methods of housekeeping, and are not less liberal and hospitable than their European fellow-colonists'.

Even without knowing the background of the authors, and allowing for the special pleading inherent in such a tract, there is still a sense that the authors have a great respect for many of the attributes of Western society, and especially those of Britain; and an equal respect for the characteristics of Chinese culture.

Ah Mouy and Kong Meng arrived within two years of each other in 1851 and 1853.[29] Ah Mouy claimed that he was first to start the Chinese goldrush to Victoria. A native of Guangdong, he came to Melbourne via Singapore, as a carpenter working with an English captain bringing prefabricated houses to Melbourne from Singapore.[30] Kong Meng was born in Penang, of a Cantonese father and a Malaysian mother. An uncle was a lawyer in the British courts in Singapore, and his brother was killed in 'the Chinese war' in the service of the East India Company (this was probably the First Opium War).[31] In 1859, Kong Meng argued in court in Melbourne that he need not pay the Chinese residence tax as, being born in a British colony, he was a British subject — although the court determined that 'the mere fact of Kong Meng having been born in a British settlement did not constitute him a British subject, without collateral evidence of his parents being British subjects also'.[32]

Both built their fortunes on a combination of trading and investing in gold mining.[33] Both imported Chinese foodstuffs for their fellow immigrants, and tea for the British Australians.[34] Kong Meng had his own fleet of six ships and traded across the Indian Ocean and in South-East Asia.[35] Each had substantial investments in companies with a majority of British Australian directors.[36] They were not exclusive denizens of the Chinese quarter, but mixed in the leading business and social circles of Melbourne.[37] They were also at the forefront of economic innovation, being pioneers in coal mining for the new steam ships and refrigerated fishing boats for the Bass Strait fleets.[38] Both were foundation members of the Commercial Bank of Australia in 1866, and were among its largest shareholders.[39] Throughout the 19th century, when Australian private banks printed their own notes, this bank printed Chinese text on its notes, and possibly also a series with German text, both in general circulation.[40] Both actions were an acknowledgement of the considerable populations of Chinese and Germans in the colony,[41] and clearly indicate a willingness to accommodate and incorporate non-British cultures into the economic and cultural development of the country. Kong Meng also organised displays at various Melbourne International Exhibitions of Chinese crafts and industry.[42] Ah Mouy, a leading member of the See Yup Society, donated the land for the society's elaborate temple in South Melbourne,[43] which was constructed in 1866. It still stands in Raglan Street, South Melbourne, and is a striking combination of neo-classical and Chinese design.

It is important to note that these two merchants came to Australia by way of the British Straits Settlements in South-East Asia and were engaged in commercial activities — before they arrived in Australia — which made use of the expanding operations of the British Empire in the Far East and the Indies, as well as the networks of Chinese trade. They were active at a time when Australia was still being explored and settled by the British and at a time when Britain was establishing colonial presences in China, South-East Asia, Melanesia and northern Australia, and when Chinese *émigrés* were also expanding labour and trading endeavours in the Pacific and the Indies. It was a time when the definition of Australia as being separate from Asia had not yet been made, and when many Europeans felt that the north of Australia, like New Guinea and the Indies, was better suited to people used to working in the tropics. By their operations and careers, as well as their words, Lowe Kong Meng and Louis Ah Mouy, in concert with the younger Cheong Cheok Hong, demonstrated a clear commitment to a vision of Australia which was multicultural and internationalist, with a free movement of people, a sense of hospitality and welcome, and the creation of a society combining the best of many cultures.

It is also clear, from the way immigration policy developed later in Australia, that they failed in this endeavour.

Footnotes

1. Unsourced news article on page 51 of an album of newspaper clippings regarding Lowe Kong Meng, donated to the Chinese Museum by descendants of Lowe Kong Meng. Probably dated from the 1870s.

2. Statistics for the Colony of Victoria 1858 and 1859 record Chinese population on the Victorian goldfields for 31 December, 1858 and 31 December, 1859 as 33,673 and 26,044 respectively. During 1858–59 the Victorian Government was imposing heavy discriminatory poll taxes, miners' licences and residence taxes on Chinese, and the Chinese miners were engaged in widespread evasion of these taxes. It is assumed that this evasion would have led to under-counting of the Chinese population, so it may be that numbers reached the 50,000 level. *Statistics for the Colony of Victoria 1858*, p.77, Victorian Public Records Office VPRS/943/P000 Unit 9; *Statistics for the Colony of Victoria 1859*, p.101, Victorian Public Records Office VPRS/943/P000 Unit 11.

3. Ryan, J. 1995. *Ancestors: Chinese in Colonial Australia.* p.162. Western Australia: Fremantle Arts Centre Press.

4. The 1947 Census recorded 12,094 people living in Australia whose country of origin was China (of either 'full-blood' or 'half-caste' status). See Palfreeman, A.C. 1967. *The Administration of the White Australia Policy.* pp.145–6. Melbourne: Melbourne University Press. Cited in Markus, A. 1994. *Australian Race Relations 1788–1993.* p.152. Sydney: Allen & Unwin.

5. The *English and Chinese Advertiser* was published every Saturday and delivered free of charge to all stores and places of business in the township, Main Road, Specimen Hill, Eureka, and at the stores of the Chinese at the Chinese quarters in Golden Point, Redhill and Sailors Gully. At least 96 issues were published. At that time there were approximately 5,000 Chinese living in Ballarat. Four editions are held in the Ballarat Gold Museum. The earliest surviving edition is called the *CHINESE ADVERTISER and Pioneer of Christianity and Christian Civilisation Around the Chinese in Australia.* A later three editions, called *The English and Chinese Advertiser*, are: No. 3, Saturday 25 October, 1856; No. 60, Saturday 28 November, 1857; and 7 August, 1858 (edition number illegible — may be No. 96.). A fifth edition, No. 87, Saturday 5 June, 1858, is held by the State Library of Victoria. The other extant edition is 14 March, 1857, held at the Mitchell Library in Sydney. An article in *The Argus*, 31 October, 1868, p.5, states, 'Chinese newspapers in Victoria are not wholly unknown. They have been attempted more

than once, but we believe the only success achieved in this direction was by a Mr Bell, of Ballarat. He was then a tolerable Chinese scholar, and for years printed and published upon Bakery-hill a Chinese paper. It was entirely his own affair, for he cut the characters on blocks of wood, from which he took impressions. The thing was but a rude broadsheet, after all, and died a natural death long since'.

6 *The Argus*, 31 October, 1868, p.5. The article states that 'the first number was printed and published yesterday by Mr E. Whitehead, of 87 Collins Street East ... It resembles as nearly as possible an English commercial paper, the reading matter and advertisements being, of course, compiled and edited for Chinese readers exclusively. No. 1 consists — we are informed — of a preface; a portion of the Rev Young's Chinese report; an epitome of the late mail news; an account of the late South American earthquakes; and other intelligence. The price is 6d. per copy. The *Fi-pao* office is at 75 Chancery Lane'.

7 Published in Sydney from 1894 to 1923. It is archived at the Mitchell Library, Sydney.

8 Also published in Sydney, first as the *Tung Wah News* (1898–1902) and then changing its name to the *Tung Wah Times* (1902–36). More information about this newspaper, and an index to its contents, can be found at the web site of the Chinese Heritage of Australian Federation Project, www.chaf.lib.latrobe.edu.au

9 As well as the *Chinese Australian Herald* and the *Tung Wah News/Times*, the other main newspapers were the *Chinese Times* and the *Chinese Republic News*. The *Chinese Times* was published in Melbourne from 1902 to 1922, with various changes to its Chinese name, and in its ownership and political affiliations, during the period. In 1922 the paper was transferred from Melbourne to Sydney. Although it occasionally suspended publication, it continued in print until the close of World War II. Copies of the Melbourne editions are archived at the State Library of Victoria. It is not known whether copies of the Sydney editions still exist. The *Chinese Republic News*, dating from 1912 to at least 1937, was published in Sydney. Editions for 1914 to 1937 are archived at the Mitchell Library. Besides these general newspapers a number of other Chinese-language magazines were published in Melbourne and Sydney. The Chinese Masonic Association (*Zhigongtang*), for example, issued a purely commercial magazine known as *The Bulletin* (*Gongbao*). Another was called *Harmony* (*Pingbao*) and a third *Commerce* (*Shangbao*), which was

published jointly in English and Chinese. For a summary of Australian Chinese newspapers at the turn of the 20th century, see Liu, Weiping, *Chinese Newspapers in Australia from the Turn of the Century*, which can be found at www.chaf.lib.latrobe.edu.au/chinese_newspapers.shtml. This is a translated excerpt from Liu, Weiping. 1989. *Aozhou huaqiao shi (History of Overseas Chinese in Australia)*. pp.99–105. Chapter 7. Xingdao chubanshe.

10 For an account of the development of Chinese-language newspapers in South-East Asia, see Chen, Mong Hock. 1967. *The Early Chinese Newspapers of Singapore, 1881–1912*. Singapore: University of Malaya Press.

11 Shen, Yuan Fang. 2001. *Dragon Seed in the Antipodes: Chinese-Australian Autobiographies*. Melbourne: Melbourne University Press.

12 Jong, Ah Siug, Ruth Moore and John Tully. 2000. *A Difficult Case: an autobiography of a Chinese miner on the Central Victorian goldfields*. Daylesford: Jim Crow Press.

13 Foon Kee Collection, Chinese Museum, Melbourne.

14 Donated to the Chinese Museum in 1988.

15 Frost, Warwick. 2002. Migrants and technological transfer: Chinese farming in Australia, 1850–1920. *Australian Economic History Review*. pp.113-30. Vol. 42. No. 2. July 2002.

16 Hayes, James. 1995. 'Good Morning Mrs Thomson!': a Chinese-English word-book from 19th century Sydney. In Macgregor, Paul (ed.), 1995, *Histories of the Chinese in Australasia and the South Pacific*. pp.113–26. Melbourne: Museum of Chinese Australian History.

17 The title of this paper is drawn from a petition dated 15 September, 1857, regarding the 'Influx of the Chinese', presented to members of the Legislative Assembly of Victoria. Victorian Parliamentary paper. E. 76, 1856–7.

18 This index can be viewed at the Golden Dragon Museum in Bendigo.

19 McWaters, V. 2002. *Beechworth's Little Canton: The History of the Spring Creek Chinese Camp and its Residents*. Beechworth, Victoria: self-published.

20 Images of Chinese in Australia, New Zealand and South-East Asia, 1850–1950. 2002–05. Australian Research Council Linkages Project. No. LP0211909.

21 Letter from Cheong, Cheok Hong, to unknown respondent, 19 July, 1887, which is a report on a recent Tour of Inspection in the Mission Districts of Blackwood, Daylesford, Maryborough and St Arnaud and Melbourne. Archived in the C.H. Cheong letters file, Cheong Collection, at the Chinese Museum, Melbourne.

22 Young, Rev W. 1868. Report on the condition of the Chinese population in Victoria. Presented to both Houses of Parliament in 1868. p.21. *Votes and Proceedings, Victorian Legislative Assembly.* Vol. III.

23 Oddie, G. 1962. The Lower Class Chinese and the Merchant Elite in Victoria, 1870–1890. pp.65–70. *Historical Studies.* Vol. 10.

24 Cronin, Kathryn. 1982. *Colonial Casualties: Chinese in Early Victoria.* For Kong Meng, see pp.26–31. For Ah Mouy, see pp.26–28. For Cheong, see p.117. Melbourne: Melbourne University Press.

25 L. Kong Meng, Cheong Cheok Hong and Louis Ah Mouy. 1879. *The Chinese Question in Australia, 1878–79.* Melbourne: F.F. Bailliere. An original copy of this pamphlet is held in the State Library of Victoria. A digital transcript is also available on the Chinese Heritage of Australian Federation web site, www.chaf.lib.latrobe.edu.au (Digitised Historic Documents Database in the Resources section of the site).

26 McCormack, Terri. 1988. Lowe Kong Meng, 1831–1888: Champion of racial tolerance. In Baldwin, Suzy (ed.), 1988, *Unsung Heroes and Heroines of Australia.* p.58. Greenhouse Publications.

27 Welch, I. 1997. Cheok Hong Cheong, 1851–1928. In *St Mark's Review.* p.23. Spring 1997.

28 L. Kong Meng, Cheong Cheok Hong and Louis Ah Mouy. 1879. *The Chinese Question in Australia, 1878–79.* Melbourne: F.F. Bailliere. p.1 of digital version at www.chaf.lib.latrobe.edu.au. References in the remainder of this paragraph and in the subsequent eight paragraphs are to pp.1, 3, 5 and 8 of this document.

29 Yong, Ching-fatt. 1974. Lowe Kong Meng and Louey Ah Mouy. *Australian Dictionary of Biography.* Vol. 5. Melbourne.

30 In Days of Old; Victoria's First Chinaman; Story of the Gold Fever; One Letter Brings 37,000 immigrants. p.5. *The Sun,* 12 May, 1918.

31 District Court report. *The Argus,* 3 June, 1859. Melbourne.

32 Ibid.

33 For Ah Mouy's trading and mining, see his obituary: In Days of Old; Victoria's First Chinaman; Story of the Gold Fever; One Letter Brings 37,000 immigrants. p.5. *The Sun,* 12 May, 1918. For Kong Meng's trading and mining, see Yong, Ching-fatt. 1974. Lowe Kong Meng. *Australian Dictionary of Biography.* Vol. 5. Melbourne.

34 In a meeting with the Chief Secretary of Victoria in 1859, Kong Meng is said to have just had a cargo of 10,000 pounds sterling arrived from China ('Chinese Residence Tax'. *The Examiner,* 4 June, 1859). *The Argus,* 16 February, 1874, reported: 'The ship Rifleman,

from Hong Kong, with a general cargo, consisting of rice, tea and chow-chow, consigned to Messrs. Kong Meng and Co., paid her first visit to this port yesterday'. In 1881, Kong Meng imported substantial quantities of tea on the SS *Ocean*, SS *Meath* and the SS *Bowen*, from Foochow and Hong Kong (LKM newsclippings scrapbook, Chinese Museum, pp.74, 84). Ah Mouy established a tea merchant's business in Swanston Street in 1852, which was still in business at the time of his death in 1918 (*The Sun*, 12 May, 1918. p.5).

35 Yong, Ching-fatt. 1974. Lowe Kong Meng. *Australian Dictionary of Biography*. Vol. 5. Melbourne.

36 Various news clippings documenting the affairs of Kong Meng and Ah Mouy are contained in a scrapbook of clippings donated to the Chinese Museum by descendants of Lowe Kong Meng. Ah Mouy and Kong Meng were shareholders and members of the provisional committee for the Commercial Bank of Australia, founded in 1866 (Prospectus for the Commercial Bank of Australia, *The Age*, 30 March, 1866, in scrapbook, p.18). Kong Meng was treasurer and provisional director for the Yarra Distillery Company (scrapbook, p.74). He was on the Provisional Committee for the South Crinoline Amalgamated Quartz-Mining Company (p.77), and was a provisional director of the English, Australian and New Zealand Marine Insurance Company (p.78), the Midas Consols Gold-Mining Company (p.92), the Madame Bent Gold-Mining Company (p.95), and, in 1888, of the Outward Bound Consolidated Silver-Mining Company, Thackeringa, NSW (p.98). And, although Kong Meng had the largest shareholding (10 per cent) in the Madame Kong Meng Gold-Mining Company in 1887, the rest of the 26 shareholders were British or European Australians (p.82).

37 On one occasion the Mayor of Melbourne entertained the principal Chinese mercantile men resident in Melbourne in the Town Hall (LKM newsclippings scrapbook, Chinese Museum, p.47). On another occasion it was reported that 'Mr Cook, MLA, Mayor of Hotham, Mr Whiteman, MLA, Mr Kong Meng, and a large number of well-known citizens in official and mercantile positions' were present at a banquet held by John Buncle to celebrate the opening of new showrooms for his agricultural implements (scrapbook, p.53). Kong Meng was on the committee for a banquet held in honour of visiting British parliamentarian Alderman McArthur (scrapbook, p.69). Kong Meng was also a patron of an Easter Fair to raise funds for Melbourne's New Homoeopathic Hospital (scrapbook, p.86).

38 Kong Meng was a provisional director of the Hazelwood Coal-Mining Company (LKM newsclippings scrapbook, Chinese Museum, p.47) and the Mirboo Collieries' Proprietary, Gippsland (scrapbook p.94). Kong Meng and Ah Mouy were provisional directors of the Melbourne Fishmongers and Deep Sea Fishing Company (scrapbook, p.72).

39 Prospectus for the Commercial Bank of Australia, *The Age*, 30 March, 1866, in Lowe Kong Meng newsclippings scrapbook, Chinese Museum, p.18.

40 *The Sun*, 12 May, 1918. p.5: 'Years ago certain Chinese characters were printed on the bank notes, and they aroused great curiosity. This was Ah Mouy's successful device to obtain the custom of the Chinese residents of Melbourne'.

41 By the early 1860s, more than 10,000 Germans were living in Victoria. See www.heritage.vic.gov.au/pdfforms/german_report_pp.1-21.pdf

42 McCormack, Terri. 1988. Lowe Kong Meng, 1831–1888: Champion of racial tolerance. In Baldwin, Suzy (ed.), 1988, *Unsung Heroes and Heroines of Australia*. p.57. Greenhouse Publications.

43 *The Sun*, 12 May, 1918. p.5.

3. AUSTRALIAN LOVERS
CHINGCHONG CHINAMAN, CHINESE IDENTITY AND HYBRID CONFUSION

Kam Louie

Since 1960 I have been fascinated by this topic — 'as others see us' — as a result of a bizarre childhood experience in the streets of central Sydney. I was about 10 and to this day I remember clearly the following incident: as I was walking home after school, a little boy, about six or seven, followed me for several blocks, and he kept making faces at me and calling me 'Chingchong Chinaman'. That by itself was not so unusual: I was used to such childish taunts. What shocked me then, even at such a young age, was that this little kid was himself Chinese! At that time, there were so few Chinese around that when he saw me, his reaction was to call me what others probably called him or his dad, and to see how I would respond. I will come back to this little guy later. For now, I just want to say that what he did had a tremendous impact on me. Ever since that incident, I have in one way or another been trying to find out why I was a 'Chingchong Chinaman', who I was, and how others saw me. Indeed, those of you who are familiar with my research would know that many of my publications in one way or another revolve around the issue of the Chinese identity.

My first books were about how the Chinese communists reinterpreted classical philosophers such as Confucius and Zhuangzi.[1] I wrote them because I wanted to see the methods adopted by contemporary Chinese intellectuals to remain 'Chinese' during periods when they were supposed to break completely with the past and create a new society along Marxist lines. That research was prompted as much by a desire for self-awareness — the evolving Chineseness of China — as it was by stern academic considerations. Having spent my early childhood in China, I wanted to understand the methods used by policy-makers who shaped my thinking. After I finished those books, and after the Chinese intellectuals themselves gave up the pretence that they were communists, I decided to see how they described themselves in literature. Accordingly, my next few books were about various aspects of Chinese life as described in fiction.[2] Perhaps because I was reading lots of romances and memoirs, I was soon convinced that in times of social stability the small everyday things such as the latest movie they had seen or their relationships with the opposite sex mattered most to most people. These everyday realities were as important to understanding Chineseness as the grander formal disciplines of politics, international relations or economics. My last two books were therefore about popular culture and Chinese masculinity.[3]

Note that I wrote on Chinese masculinity, not Chinese gender. I was interested in the 'man' part of the Chingchong Chinaman, not just any old Chingchong (although the fact that there was never a Chingchong Chinawoman is an interesting story in itself and relates as much to migration patterns as it does to gender non-specific language customs of the years prior to the 1970s and '80s). In the course of looking at everyday culture for these books, my focus became increasingly targeted at my immediate surroundings rather than at what was taking place in China. Those of you who have read my last book will know that I begin it by analysing traditional culture and constructions of the ideal man, but by the last two chapters, I examine the transformations of ideal Chinese masculinity in the global arena. In fact, since the book was published last year, the subject matter of my research has become even more local, because the target of analysis has recently shifted to Chinese men in Australia. I wanted to find out how Chinese men here identify themselves. I was therefore gratified to find that the National Library had a comprehensive Australiana collection in the Chinese language, expertly catalogued by Andrew Gosling and his team for ease of use. I was even more grateful and delighted when Alison invited me to this conference and sent me a bundle of documents that provided synopses of the books held in the NLA collection.

In addition to these documents, I have also had the opportunity to browse many of the books that are summarised in the Asian Accounts of Australia Project. The materials on Australia published in China and in Chinese are either very general descriptions of Australian social customs, portrayals of so-called typical Australian people, or government-generated data such as Australian spending, longevity or wealth. In addition, there are many books and pamphlets on 'big picture' domains such as the Australian political, education and welfare systems. There are also many descriptions of Australian leisure activities such as gambling and sport as well as tourist information in the form of straight picture books or travel diaries. Even though some of the customs and people described are too stereotypical for my liking, I am fully aware that such information is useful and essential for Chinese readers who want to find out about how much Australians earn, how they vote, what they need to do to get into university and so on.

My interest, however, is more in their private feelings than Australian systems, and there is relatively little on the emotional life of the Chinese themselves or descriptions of meaningful and deep relationships with other Australians. Perhaps that is fortunate, because in the time given to prepare for this conference, I would not have been able to finish many books anyway. Using the documents that Alison sent me as a guide, I read as much as I could in the given time. For those books that I have not had the time to peruse, I have relied on the summaries provided in the documents Alison sent me as well as reading tables of contents and juicy bits in selected novels. My paper is therefore only a very preliminary report, based on fictional and semi-fictional accounts by Chinese students who arrived in Australia in the late 1980s and early 1990s. I will assess how these young Chinese writers manage their love lives in Australia, and I will illustrate those observations by pointing to a few novels and short stories from collections such as *Aozhou qingren* (*Australian Lovers*).[4]

Because of time limitations, I will discuss only material written by students who came from China in the late 1980s and early 1990s. There are some stories by students from other parts of Asia. For example, two volumes of excellent stories by Melbourne University students from Hong Kong, Singapore, Taiwan as well as China have been published and their concerns are quite different.[5] I will have to wait for another occasion to look at this and other materials. Instead, I will focus on the lives of Chinese men from the People's Republic, concentrating on stories written by them. In the process, I will point to their views of Australian men and women. That is, how they see us.

I should make a couple of general remarks before proceeding. First of all, the materials summarised in this project were almost all written in the past 20 years. This is partly because the National Library is a relatively new library, with the National Library Act coming into force only in 1960, and Chinese books and serials were actively being collected only since then. We know that Chinese newspapers were published in the 19th century and John Fitzgerald and Paul McGregor have shown that even back then the Australian Chinese were keen to make sure that their Australian Chinese identity contributed to a new sense of Australian nationhood just before Federation.[6] Nevertheless, it remains a fact that most Chinese who came before the 1980s were from the peasantry, and almost all of them were men. They were seen by most Australians, including themselves, as sojourners rather than citizens. They wrote about politics, about Australia and about China, but rarely about their romantic relationships with other Australians. After 1900, the numbers of Chinese in Australia dropped, from 3.3 per cent of the population in 1861 to less than 1 per cent in 1901.[7] Furthermore, with only a few exceptions, they did not produce any fictional writing about their own lives.

The situation in the late 1980s and 1990s represents a most conspicuous break from all previous times. Alison Broinowski in her book *The Yellow Lady* aptly characterises this period in Australian history as one of hybridisation and fusion.[8] This was a time when Australia actively reoriented itself towards Asia, and when a huge influx of migrants came from Asia to make Australia their new home. For Chinese in particular, the late 1980s and early 1990s brought a completely different kind of sojourner. As a result of changes in China, and the 1989 Tiananmen incident in particular, tens of thousands of 'Chinese students' came to Australia. Whether they successfully studied here is not important for our purposes. What is important is that most of them would have finished secondary schooling in China and could read and write Chinese well. In their homelands, most of them would be considered intellectuals. They wrote and they read. And many novels and short stories were published, and were often serialised in newspapers and journals established in the past 20 years. In Sydney alone, there were at least four Chinese daily newspapers, four weekly magazines and numerous journals in the 1990s.[9] There were also specialist literary journals, such as *Otherland*, which was established in 1996 in Melbourne. Even here in Canberra, a Chinese literary journal, *Kanjing wenyuan* (*Canberra Literati*), was established in June 2002.

These new migrants are very different to those who came before in other ways. Unlike previous periods, such as the beginning of the century, when the ratio of Chinese men to women was 61.5 to 1, men and women are almost equally represented. Similarly, unlike earlier periods, when romantic and sexual liaisons between themselves and other Australians were rare or sanctioned, they are now a central concern, so you can say that my research is not quirky or kinky, but timely and necessary. In fact, in the introduction to their translations of two novellas written in 1991, Bruce Jacobs and Ouyang Yu observe that these novels broke new ground by 'referring to the sexual needs of people far from home and families'.[10] Love and sex might have been a novelty in Chinese Australian writing in 1991, but by the mid to late 1990s, sex and love were such common themes in memoirs and fiction that the novel *Meng de yaoshi*,[11] which should be translated as *The Key to Dream*, has been incorrectly but understandably mistranslated by the research assistants of the Asian Accounts of Australia Project as *The Key to Love*.

Incidentally, the author of one of these early novels, *My Fortune in Australia*, repeatedly makes the claim that 'Chinese-Australians had formed an indissoluble bond with Australia', and that ancient Chinese books had reported the Chinese seeing kangaroos and boomerangs as early as 338 BC.[12] The suggestion that Australia is somehow connected to the Chinese in the mists of time is beautifully made in one of my favourite stories from the collection *Australian Lovers*.

Strange Encounter is written in the style of traditional ghost stories in which the Chinese girlfriend of the protagonist, by the name of Su Shan, leaves him. In despair, he drives in the middle of nowhere and meets a beautiful young woman called Susan. They go diving into an underwater cave and there they find a skeleton. The skeleton has a ring on her finger, with the name 'Susan' engraved on it. Using this ring, the young couple vow that they will get married and proceed to make love. It turns out that even though Susan is a fair-dinkum, blonde-haired Aussie, her great-grandfather was Chinese and so in the distant past, she was somehow Chinese. In keeping with the traditional 'strange tales', the narrator discovers some days afterwards that the skeletal Susan was in fact the same Susan that he made love to, a girl who was drowned while diving.[13] There is more to this story and I'll come back to it later.

The second general observation I should make is that most of the works I am discussing today were originally written in Chinese for Chinese readers. They therefore present images the authors want Chinese readers to see. In recent years, many popular books have been published in English describing happy white-Asian marital relations. Curiously, most of these books are written by Asian women. In a review of recent best-sellers by authors such as Nien Cheng, Jung Chang, Aiping Mu and Anhua Gao, the *Far Eastern Economic Review* points out that these Chinese women writers have been successful because they have stuck to the formula: 'A young woman struggles but survives the Cultural Revolution in China ... to find health, happiness — and a husband — in the West'. The reviewer argues that these heart-breaking memoirs pander to Western preconceptions, whereby 'Red China is the evil enemy that treats its people like beasts, denying them freedom and happiness, which can only be found in the West'.[14] In these popular memoirs and novels, the saviour husbands are always white and their wives Chinese.

As some of you would know, the idea that in matters of sex and love Asian men are not as good as white men is not restricted to English materials written by Asian women living abroad. In the 1980s, Chinese women writers in China, such as Zhang Jie, alleged that Chinese men were becoming effeminate and that there were no real men in China any more. In 1994, a Chinese woman, Shi Guoying, created a huge controversy in Sydney when she publicly proclaimed that, based on personal experience, Chinese men were incompetent lovers compared with white men.[15] The claim that Chinese men have no balls was alarming to many Chinese men who spent years navel-gazing and soul-searching trying to make sense of their masculine identities. It is in such a climate that Chinese Australian men write about their own identities and how those identities relate to 'ours', that is, the 'Australian Australians'.

The concept of 'identity' is one which has been discussed *ad nauseam* in philosophy, cultural studies, gender studies, diaspora and Australian studies. It is also one of the central preoccupations of the characters in 1990s Australian Chinese fiction. The Chinese for 'identity' in philosophical and academic discourse is probably best translated as '*benti*'. For example, I have written mainly on how the Chinese see themselves as communists when they have the burden of a long and resilient Confucian heritage to carry around. The abstract concept of Chinese identity is in this case appropriately translated as *benti*. In the literature we are looking at here, however, the term used is '*shenfen*', a much more concrete and important idea. *Shenfen* is literally one's status. That status can refer to things such as class or generational background. Most importantly, in the case of Chinese Australian literature, it is one's nationality or residence status. Thus, in many stories, the characters' main preoccupation is to get themselves *shenfen*, that is to say, to get themselves permanent residence status in Australia, preferably to acquire Australian citizenship.

The struggle to obtain this legal residential status is central to the lives of the Chinese characters in the stories I have read. In order to convey this concern to their readers, one author has titled her semi-autobiographical novel *Green Card Dreams*,[16] because most Chinese readers, indeed most readers throughout the world, would be familiar with the phrase 'Green Card', although such a card does not exist in Australia. This is illustrated by the frontispiece of the book itself. Here, the author displays her driver's licence, her NRMA membership card, her Advance Bank card, her Sydney University student's card and even her childcare card. But no green card. In any case, being able to live here permanently is to have *shenfen*. As the protagonist of the novel *Broken Clouds* observes, 'There is only one thing in life — your *shenfen*, once you have that, you have everything'.[17] And this is how these student writers see us, the Australians. It doesn't matter if we are of British, Italian, Korean, French or Chinese background, we have a *shenfen*, an identity.

We are indeed a lucky country, because our identity is precisely what these newcomers want. And they will do anything to get it. I will give a typical example from the literature we are considering. It is important to note here that much of this literature is autobiographical/biographical, so there is often a blurring of what real students are after in contemporary Australian society and what their characters are after in literary texts. The 1995 novel *Broken Clouds* is about a young man, Meng Long, who leaves his wife in China to come to Australia. She has an affair and leaves him. He and another Chinese student in Australia become lovers. But she has no status and she also leaves him to marry an old white Australian who has *shenfen*. In despair, he courts his white English teacher, by the name of Jennifer, in order to get *shenfen*. When Jennifer finds out that it's not her body and mind, but her *shenfen*, that he is really after, she also leaves him. His visa runs out and he gets very drunk on the evening before he boards the plane for China. He collapses on the plane and has to return to Melbourne. At this juncture, then Immigration Minister Nick Bolkus announces an amnesty for all the Chinese students who arrived in Australia before 20 June, 1989. The novel finishes with Meng Long getting his *shenfen*.

As lovers, Australians do very well. Contrary to the myth that Chinese men see Australian women as plastic, promiscuous Playboy pin-up types, Jennifer is a fairly ordinary woman, who, like everybody else, just wants a fulfilling life. By contrast, the Chinese wife and the Chinese lover abandon the protagonist because he has no *shenfen*. The *shenfen*-hungry Chinese woman is even more vividly illustrated in the novel *Bungee-Jumping in Australia*, written five years after *Broken Clouds* by the same author, Liu Ao.[18] By this stage the author has Australian citizenship, and his protagonist Wu Ming likewise has *shenfen*. He goes back to China, looking for a wife. His ex-wife, whose lover has by this stage discarded her, tries to reunite with him but he declines. One after another, the women he is matched up with are after only one thing, his *shenfen*. Like the monk Tripitaka in the novel *Journey to the West*, he is deceived by these good-looking demon women, all eager to devour him in order to change their *shenfen* status. But he manages to rebuff them all.

This second novel is in many ways more mature and informative than the first. It is deliberately constructed so that comparisons between China and Australia are made. Issues such as education, welfare, multiculturalism and sexual morality are discussed. On the whole, Australia compares very well with China. In terms of how the Chinese see us, the good and bad aspects of Australia are shown. On love and marriage, for example, one central character, Susan, is a white Australian who loves Chinese culture so much she goes to Taiwan and then to the mainland, and falls in love with a Chinese man who is a nasty gangster cum businessman type. As a result, her white Australian husband, who is a successful doctor, divorces her and forms a white supremacist political party. The novel ends with this doctor hooking up with the young Chinese air-hostess who Wu Ming loves and sponsors to Australia. And the old white supremacist and the young Chinese woman drive off together into the sunset.

Interestingly, many of the novels I have read in this collection suggest that it is the Chinese women who will use you for your *shenfen*, and then dump you. Thus, in the story *Strange Encounter* mentioned earlier, it is the Chinese girlfriend Su Shan who leaves the protagonist, and the Australian Susan who marries him, even in death. Another good illustration of how Chinese men resent or fear Chinese women can be seen in the story *The Chaos of Love*.[19] The narrator leaves his girlfriend behind in China and comes to Australia. He meets and marries a Filipina sex worker and goes with her back to her poverty-stricken village to find that his background is superior to hers in every way. His Chinese girlfriend still writes to him and assumes they will get together somehow. But in the end the narrator decides to stay with the Filipina because he likes the fact that she is compliant. He concludes that the Filipina wife is better because his Chinese girlfriend is 'ambitious', and that if she comes to Australia, she is likely to surpass him in achieving and leave him. There is certainly strong evidence that the misogyny so strong in traditional Chinese society is still alive and well today, even in Australia.

In any case, *shenfen* does not solve everything. Once the Chinese students have that *shenfen*, they find that love and life continue to be confusing and unpredictable. It is, of course, not all bad news. One aspect of Australian society that is considered good by all is multiculturalism. As I have shown elsewhere, one of the most endearing stories from a volume of self-confessions by Chinese students writing in Australia, titled *I Married A Foreigner*, is by the editor of that collection.[20] He wanted desperately to marry an Australian. In the end, he does so, and that Australian is of Korean background. They were both foreigners in Australia, and now they are both Australians. The love stories in the collection are roughly divided into two parts: those that involve Chinese-Chinese partnerships and those that are Chinese-Foreigners. In this case, 'foreigners' means Australians of Korean, Italian or French descent and so on. Most of the Chinese-Chinese partnerships fail and the Chinese-Foreigner ones succeed.

If these self-confessions are any guide, they do show that to some lovers at least, the perception of Australia in the 1990s is that this is a society in which hybridity and fusion have been achieved with relative success. There are still many problems and challenges ahead, but at least now the typical Australian is no longer confined to the bright and white Vegemites described by advertisers or One Nation propagandists. Or, worse still, by the narrator, Nino Culotta, in the 1957 novel *They're A Weird Mob*, by Irish Australian John O'Grady, who opined that:

> *There is no better way of life in the world than that of the Australian. I firmly believe this. The grumbling, growling, cursing, profane, laughing, beer drinking, abusive, loyal-to-his-mates Australian is one of the few free men left on this earth. He fears no one, crawls to no one, bludges on no one, and acknowledges no master. Learn his way. Learn his language. Get yourself accepted as one of him; and you will enter a world that you never dreamed existed. And once you have entered it, you will never leave it.*[21]

As one critic of the highly acclaimed 1963 movie based on the novel astutely observed, 'We multicultural Australians now consider this film to be simple-minded and banal. And bogus, after all the scriptwriter and the original author both used pseudonyms ... Ultimately the film seems all rather sad. The issues of immigration and assimilation are not very funny. It is incomprehensible the hero could forsake a rich Italian culture to the mindless, hedonistic, hyper-materialistic lifestyle presented.'[22] Fortunately, with the widespread acceptance of multiculturalism by the turn of the century, Australia has irretrievably and fundamentally changed.

We now see others with different eyes. And, in turn, others look at us with different eyes. Most importantly, we see ourselves with different eyes. One good illustration of that comes from the 1996 movie *Floating Life*, made by the Hong Kong-Australian director Clara Law. Instead of the usual Chinatown backdrop, Law goes into the suburbs. Chinese, like most Australians, live in suburbs. Chinatowns, like the outback, are enjoyed mostly by tourists who just want a bit of the Other.[23] The sophistication of Law's depiction of a Hong Kong migrant family living in the Australian suburbs provides multiple angles of Australians as being a multi-focal culture when it comes to looking at ourselves.

Indeed, in the stories I have looked at, there is a pronounced progression of how the writers see us, the Australians. From simple stereotypes, they now view us with a mixture of love, hate, admiration, contempt, mindfulness and bewilderment. In short, all the feelings we have of ourselves. In a curious sort of way, my own journey of self-discovery began in Chinese studies, where I studied Chinese culture in China. I finish up, however, by looking at the Chinese in Australia and talking to Australian studies colleagues such as David Carter. As Ann Curthoys has observed, the Australian story is also part of the Chinese Australian story.[24]

This hybridity and interdisciplinarity does not come without some initial confusion and soul-searching. I cite the example of two academic colleagues who many of you would know. The first is Ien Ang, whose essay *On Not Speaking Chinese* captures the feeling of many whom are racially Chinese but who are brought up almost totally outside of the Chinese cultural sphere.[25] But their looks make them exotic and it is expected that they should also have an exotic culture. This cultural baggage is hoisted on their shoulders and imposes a burden on them although the baggage may be empty. Of more interest is Allan Luke, former Dean of Education at Queensland University. He is more interesting because Allan is a man and that is what interests me here today. Even though he is a very successful man in Australian society, in one revealing essay he describes how when 'looking in the mirror, we find ourselves without any of the characteristics of dominant masculinity — white skin, hairy chests, beards and facial hair, big arms and big muscles'.[26] Allan was born and brought up in California so his upbringing was mostly American; he studied in Canada and has lived for many years in Queensland. There is thus little that is culturally Chinese in his background. Yet, in Australian public discourses on masculine ideals, Asian men like him are defined in terms of absence.

Who are 'we' and who are the 'others'? How do we look at others? And how do others see us? Most importantly, how do we see ourselves? With or without *shenfen*, our self-identity is constantly being challenged and remade. One interesting example is provided by the novel *The Eastern Slope Chronicle*, published only last year.[27] Though written in English, the author, Ouyang Yu, does publish plenty in Chinese and is well-represented in the collection we are considering. The novel is about one of the students who came to Australia in the late 1980s, who has since become an Australian citizen and who returns to his home town. He gets a job at his former university and gives lectures about Australia. He is known as 'the Australian', yet he and some of his friends and students are confused and bemused by this identity.

Although Alison Broinowski is correct to point out that writings such as this show that Chinese Australian men 'remain angry and humiliated, as if desexed by the experience of diaspora',[28] I also sense that throughout the novel the main concern of this intelligent and educated man is to find his identity. In Australia, he is legally an Australian, but he is perceived as Chinese. He is pseudo-Australian. In China, he is also legally Australian, but people perceive him as fake. He speaks Chinese fluently, yet he is not Chinese. He is pseudo-Chinese. No wonder he remains angry.

Here I want to return to the little Chinese boy who followed me around the streets of Sydney taunting me and calling me 'Chingchong Chinaman'. I subsequently got to know who he was: he was born in Australia and knew no Chinese. I think his parents also knew very little Chinese. He was ignorant. He was insecure. He was confused. He was looking for someone to blame for his fears. He was racist. He had, as Nino Cullota of *They're A Weird Mob* exhorted, learnt the Australian language, a language which at that time included 'Chingchong Chinaman' as a keyword in its vocabulary. That little boy reflected general Australian attitudes at the time. I hope that by now he has come to realise that Nino Cullota, or John O'Grady speaking through Nino, was wrong. Learning the language and the way of 'the Australian' then did not necessarily mean you were accepted. There was more chance of me accepting that little guy than any Cullota or O'Grady.

Now, more than 40 years later, I am sure he would be less confused and see himself as Australian. That is, he is one of 'us'. To repeat a cliché, we are many, we are one, we are Australians. Certainly, despite their ethnicity, most of the authors I have discussed today are also Australian. I chose to look at their views on things such as love, sex and marriage because they are what make us human. In this, I have found that much of what is said about us is what we say about ourselves. There are, of course, some differences, most significantly the language used and the feeling that there is another home apart from home here. These issues are also important, as the concerns about citizenship show. These differences, however, are bound to disappear. In the late 20th century, the Chinese Australian identity was very much bound up with *shenfen*. My guess is that in the 21st century identity issues surrounding the Chinese Australian will merge and fuse with a general search for an Australian national identity.

In fact, in the study *Living Diversity: Australia's Multicultural Future*, which was reported in the *Sydney Morning Herald* on 25 November, 2002, of some 3,500 people from non-English backgrounds (not Chinese, though) surveyed, 10 per cent thought themselves Australians compared with 30 per cent of second-generation migrants.[29] That is not an incredible figure. But it is a 200 per cent increase in one generation. The little boy who followed me was third-generation. If the acceptance rate continues at 200 per cent, there is a 90 per cent chance that he would consider himself Australian, as shown by his reaction to me. Although I was born in China, my grandfather and father came to Australia when they were young men, so I am sort of a pseudo-third generation as well. The boy was correct to see me as a reflection of himself. And he was probably trying hard, like myself, to figure out what this 'Chingchong Chinaman' meant. I hope that he has since discovered the answer. I can't provide a definitive answer, yet. But I do know that when we look into the question of how others see us, we often end up with a picture that is exactly the same as 'how we see ourselves'.

Footnotes

1. See Louie, Kam. 1986. *Inheriting Tradition: Interpretations of the Classical Philosophers in Communist China, 1949–1966*. Oxford University Press. And Louie, Kam, 1980, *Critiques of Confucius in Contemporary China*. Hong Kong: Chinese University Press.
2. See, for example, Louie, Kam. 1989. *Between Fact and Fiction: Essays on Post-Mao Chinese Literature and Society*. Sydney: Wild Peony Press. And Louie, Kam and Bonnie McDougall. 1997. *The Literature of China in the Twentieth Century*. New York: Columbia University Press.
3. Louie, Kam. 2002. *Theorising Chinese Masculinity: Society and Gender in China*. Cambridge University Press. Louie, Kam and Bob Hodge. 1998. *The Politics of Chinese Language and Culture*. London: Routledge.
4. Zhang Wei and A Niu (eds). 1998. *Aozhou qing ren: Aodaliya Zhongguo liuxuesheng qing'ai xiaoshuo xuan (Australian Lovers: A Selection of Australian Chinese International Students' Love Stories)*. Nanchang: Baihuazhou wenyi chubanshe.
5. Chinese Writers' Association of Melbourne. 1996. *Nan shiji xing xia (Under the Southern Cross)*. Melbourne: Aodaliya Mo'erben daxue zhonghua chubanshe. Chen Suyuan, Huang Zhongyuan and Guo Weiying (eds). 1998. *Xinling shafayi (A Couch for the Soul)*. Melbourne: Aodaliya Mo'erben daxue zhonghua chubanshe.
6. Fitzgerald, John. Visions of Australian Federation: the View from the Chinese Press Gallery. In Chan, Henry, Ann Curthoys and Nora Chiang (eds), 2001, *The Overseas Chinese in Australasia: History, Settlement and Interactions*. pp.102–16. Taipei: Interdisciplinary Group for Australian Studies, National Taiwan University and Canberra: Centre for the Study of the Chinese Southern Diaspora, Australian National University. See also Paul Macgregor's paper in this volume.
7. Inglis, Christine. 1999. Australia. In Pan, Lynn (ed.), 1999, *The Encyclopedia of the Chinese Overseas*. p.274. Richmond: Curzon Press.
8. Broinowski, Alison. 1996 edition. *The Yellow Lady: Australian Impressions of Asia*. pp.216–31. Oxford University Press.
9. Zhang Wei. 1998. Xu (Preface). In *Australian Lovers*. p.3.
10. Jacobs, J. Bruce and Ouyang Yu (translated and introduced by). 1995. Introduction. *Bitter Peaches and Plums: Two Chinese Novellas on the Recent Chinese Student Experience in Australia*. p.v. Clayton, Victoria: Monash Asia Institute.
11. Chen Aizhen. 1998. *Meng de yaoshi (The Key to a Dream)*. Beijing: Zhongguo wenlian chubangongsi.

12 Liu Guande. 1995. My Fortune in Australia. pp.13–14. In *Bitter Peaches and Plums*.
13 Wen Tao. 1998. Qi yuan (Strange Encounter). pp.171–213. In *Australian Lovers*.
14 Yoon, Suh-kyung. 2001. The Crying Game. *Far Eastern Economic Review*. p.66. Vol. CLXIV 14.
15 For a summary of this controversy, see Yong Zhong. 2001. What's Behind White Masks and Yellow Skin: A Postcolonial Critique of a Chinese Sex Debate in Sydney. In Ommundsen, Wenche, 2001, *Bastard Moon: Essays on Chinese-Australian Writing*. Special Issue of *Otherland*. p.57–72. No. 7.
16 Bi Xiyan. 1996. *Lü ka meng (Green Card Dreams)*. Beijing: Huaxia chubanshe.
17 Liu Ao. 1995. *Yun duan Aozhou lu (Broken Clouds: The Australian Road)*. p.246. Beijing: Qunzhong chubanshe.
18 Liu Ao. 1999. *Bengji Aozhou (Bungee-Jumping in Australia)*. Beijing: Qunzhong chubanshe. The project assistants have translated the title as *To Furthest Australia*. My translation conveys more of the intent of the novel.
19 Sheng Yaohua. 1997. Ai zhi mang (The Chaos of Love). In *Yuanxiang (Otherland)*. pp.45–57. No. 3.
20 Louie, Kam. 2001. I Married a Foreigner: Recovering Chinese Masculinity in Australia. In *Bastard Moon*. pp.39–56.
21 Culotta, Nino (John O'Grady). 1957. *They're A Weird Mob*. p.204. Sydney: Ure Smith.
22 Matheson, Mark. A View from Australia. *The Powell & Pressburger Pages*. http://www.powell-pressburger.org/Reviews/66_Weird/Weird04.html
23 See my critique of the movie in Louie, Kam, 2003, Floating Life: Nostalgia for the Confucian Patriarch in Suburban Sydney. In Berry, Chris (ed.), 2003, *New Cinema Classics in China*. London: British Film Institute.
24 Curthoys, Ann. 2001. 'Chineseness' and Australian Identity. In *The Overseas Chinese in Australasia*. pp.16–29.
25 This essay appears as the leading chapter in Ien Ang, 2001, *On Not Speaking Chinese: Living Between Asia and the West*. London: Routledge.
26 Luke, Allan. 1997. Representing and Reconstructing Asian Masculinities: This is not a Movie Review. *Social Alternatives*. p.33. XVI 31.
27 Ouyang Yu. 2002. *The Eastern Slope Chronicle*. Sydney: Brandl & Schlesinger.

[28] Broinowski, Alison. 1999. Asian-Australian Fiction. Paper presented at the Asian Australian Identities Conference, 27–29 September, 1999. http://www.anu.edu.au/asianstudies/asia_fiction.html

[29] Banham, Cynthia. 2002. Ain't Life Grand in Australia — It's a Pity We're Still Strangers. *Sydney Morning Herald*, 25 November, 2002.

4. *HAIGUI*: A KEYWORD FOR 2003

Ouyang Yu

Doing a keyword search for *haigui* (海归) at sina.com.cn, there are 3,830 entries and if you do a related keyword search for *haiguipai* (海归派) (*haigui*, group of people) at yahoo.com.cn, you'll find 3,844 entries.

Hai for 'sea' and *gui* for 'return', *haigui* is a new Chinese word combination that means a return to China from overseas. Specifically, it is a *liuxingyu* (pop term) that refers to the recent trend in which tens of thousands of Western-educated Chinese intellectuals return to China to contribute to the Motherland.

A brief history of *haigui*
In recent Chinese history, there have been three waves of *haigui*; the first in 1949 and 1950 when the New China was founded, the second in 1997 and early 2000 when the Internet craze swept through China and the third in late 2001 and the present[1] *Haigui* could be traced further back to the early 20th century when many famous writers went back to China after they completed their studies overseas, including Lu Xun (Japan), Guo Moruo (Japan), Hu Shi (the US), Lao Se (Britain), Qian Zhongshu (France) and others; the progenitors of the New Culture in China.[2]

Of the 458,000 people who went overseas after the *gaige kaifang* (reform and open-up) policy introduced at the end of the Cultural Revolution in the late 1970s, 140,000 have returned,[3] with more than 30,000 in Beijing,[4] 32,000 in Shanghai,[5] and the rest throughout the country, mainly concentrated in the coastal cities such as Shenzhen, still one of the first choices for many.[6] Another source has it that, of all the Chinese students overseas, 60 per cent have expressed their wish to go back and *fuwu* (serve) the country.[7]

In the Australian context, the *haigui* phenomenon began in the mid-1990s when most of the post-Tiananmen Square incident students secured their permanent residency in Australia and went back (most of them males) in search of wives or to bring back their families long living in separation. As far as I know, this is only temporary for they came back to Australia as soon as they achieved their purposes.

As a term, *haigui* is almost unknown in the Australian Chinese community. It was only towards the end of last year that I was made aware of it and lately I had the amusing experience of observing a number of friends mystified by its meaning when I mentioned it to them deliberately.

Why *haigui* and who *haigui*?

One of the main reasons for *haigui* cited by the China News Net (*Zhongguo Xinwenwang*) is financial. In its own words, 'There is a great *qianjing* [prospect, also money prospect] for the *haigui* wave after [China entered the] WTO,'[8] as more and more Chinese students currently studying in the US 'have gradually changed their perception that they must somehow stay for further development in the United States of America and they now regard China as an employment market with an extremely great potential'.[9]

There is financial incentive galore. The Central Government asserted that it would provide a *kuaichedao* (fast-track) for talented people overseas[10] and the core of the Government policy was 'supporting ... study overseas, encouraging a return to China and freedom of staying and leaving'.[11] In 2002, more than 20 delegations from eight provinces and cities in China went overseas to recruit students.[12]

Head-hunting for the best people, universities in Beijing, for example, offer prospective professors annual salaries in the range of 100,000 yuan (equivalent to $AUD16,000), 10 times more than a factory worker in China, plus free three-bedroom accommodation and a one-off settlement fee of 100,000 yuan and a scientific and technological research fee ranging from 100,000 to 500,000 yuan.[13] According to one source, the famed Tsinghua University in Beijing offers one million yuan ($AUD160,000) to 28 scholars from abroad as guest professors for three to four months each year working in the Economic and Management School of the university.[14]

A living example in Melbourne is a friend of mine who has recently decided to leave Australia, having quit his secure job at IBM in favour of his new position as a general manager in Shanghai. Asked why he made this decision, he said, 'I'm now in my mid-30s. It's either now or never. Australia is basically meant for the old. Instead of getting stuck in a nine-to-five job for ever without much prospect, I have a better future in China. Plus there is much more fun in Shanghai, too'.

Among those who *haigui*, there are people who are temporary visitors to Australia and elsewhere in the West. Of many I have met, there is a similar perception as expressed above: Australia is too quiet for anything. If you visit the country as a tourist, it is fine because you get nice scenic spots, great sunshine and a clean environment, but you can't rely just on those for a living. You need something more. These temporary visitors are not ordinary people; they are company executives, directors, university presidents, highly placed officers, publishers and senior editors, professors and senior engineers, who, unlike those in 1989, would not easily give up their current positions in China in favour of the so-called 'freedom' in Australia and the West. In fact, many of them have negative views about, say, America. I met a senior official from the Ministry of Finance in 1999 at a dinner at which he told me of the impressions the US left on him: 'America is a backward country. We shall beat them in 10 or 20 years'. It is a view shared by many intellectuals in China. And they often dismiss

Australia as a country whose only advantages are clean air, blue sky and little else.

It is not just business people who *haigui*. Writers do, too. In a recent interview with a mainland-based writer, it is revealed that writers have flocked back, such as Hong Ying (Britain), Yan Geling (US), Liu Suola, Zhang Xinxin, Xu Xing, Ya Ding (France) and Leslie Zhao (Australia),[15] including even those who were dissidents in the past, such as poets Huang Xiang (based in the US), who wished to go back, and Bei Dao (US), who recently went back. In the words of the well-known Chinese dissident, editor of online magazine *China Monthly*, Su Xiaokang, he is unable to 'adapt to the West' and he admits that, for him, China is still 'the source of power and artistic inspiration'.[16]

Wang Gan, editor of an anthology entitled *A Collection of* Haigui *Women Writers,* said that, in their writings, they express collisions and conflicts between Eastern and Western cultures and a more genuine consciousness of *bentu*,[17] and do not just one-sidedly try to *jiegui*[18] with, draw themselves close to and identify with the Western cultures.[19] Hong Ying put it more directly, 'China is my motherland and it is not possible not to return [to her]. There are no people who do not want to return. Temporarily living abroad is only possible because of [their] fate'.[20]

Another living example is Tang Yuanfeng, who was working in a big company in London but found it hard to be accepted because of cultural differences. At lunch-time, when everyone produced their sandwiches, he took out his lunchbox containing instant noodles, to the amazement of all his English colleagues, who made fun of him. Tang said he had got used to the Western way of working before he went to Britain but he could not possibly change his 'Chinese stomach'.[21] Cheng Jieping decided to return to China after he received his Master's degree in Law at Cambridge because he realised he would never be accepted as a Chinese by the right-leaning middle class, represented by lawyers and the like[22] in London.

However, when I told my general manager friend mentioned before of this story, he said it was not true here in

Australia. Where he worked, he drank tea while his colleagues drank coffee, both cultures coexisting without any problems. The problem, though, is his perception that the senior management is all controlled by *yingguoren* (the English people), with junior positions held by Greeks and Italians, and his realisation that as a Chinese he is never going to get beyond 'the granite ceiling'.[23]

It would be interesting to speculate whether they have been pushed back by the West or pulled back by China, or both, although being pushed back is certainly a strong feeling I got back in 1996 as I told an interviewer from the *Sydney Morning Herald*[24] and, now, I feel only unwanted by either as I age beyond my use-by date. And it would also be interesting to speculate about what loss this would bring to the Western countries where these *haiguipai* were educated and, as far as I know, the sharpest criticisms of the West often come from the *haiguipai* because they are acquainted with the dark aspects of the societies they were temporarily tied to before they severed that connection, again temporarily.

Ban haigui

Ban in Chinese means 'half' and *ban haigui*, my own coinage, means half *haigui*. In a sense, most of these *haiguipai* are *ban haigui*, such as Hong Ying, who spends six months of each year in Beijing and six in London. There is an issue of duality involved, which is that most of these *haiguipai* have one thing in common: they are citizens of other countries. Hong Ying holds a British passport and Leslie Zhao holds an Australian passport, which is very important, as a friend of mine said: 'Once there's something wrong politics-wise in China, I can exit any time I want to because I enjoy immunity as a foreign citizen'. Another friend of mine, a professor now based at Shenzhen University, decided to go back to China only after he secured his Australian permanent residency, a common practice these days.

Business people tend to be *ban haigui* as it gives them the opportunity to move between countries and cultures. It's an age-old practice by Hong Kongese and Taiwanese business people, who leave their wives and children in Australia and elsewhere to *zuo yiminjian* (sit through a migrant's prison) while they make their money at home, occasionally visiting their families overseas. These days, the practice has passed on to the mainlanders with more and more rich people sending their children to private schools in Australia and other countries,[25] among whom were some corrupt officials who laundered their money this way.

The *ban haigui* is also shown in the choice of locations. Many opt to go to Hong Kong instead of mainland China for its relative political freedom and lucrative remunerations. In 2002, I went to the Hong Kong International Literary Festival and met a number of Chinese double-exiles who had moved from Melbourne and other cities in Australia and were working in private schools in Hong Kong. One of the main reasons cited for this was a much better annual salary, equivalent to $A180,000 with a lower tax rate (about 13 per cent)!

This *ban haigui* phenomenon reflects a deep distrust among them of the potential instability of the Chinese political system and a psychological split with the West where they can't live very comfortably as intellectuals. As Hong Ying put it, she lives a 'solitary hermit's life [in London] and, apart from what I have to do to promote my books in association with my publishers in the States and Europe, I refuse to see anyone and I only stay with my family and a few very close friends'.[26] She summed it all up by saying, 'In my opinion, world culture is in a state of confrontation. Both my *Ananda* and *K* are about conflicts between Chinese and Western cultures and the difficulty to adjust. Even between lovers, communications are hard'.[27]

With Hong Kong's return in 1997 to mainland China as a symbol, the *haigui* trend can best be described as part of a centripetal force represented by the colour yellow, succinctly summarised in a song by the Hong Kong pop singer, Luo Dayou, who said, 'Don't ever forget my face that will never change its yellow colour'.[28] In this pull towards the Motherland, even those still based overseas are dubbed *haiguipai* writers, such as Zhang Ling,[29] a Canada-based woman writer, and Yan Geling, because they write in Chinese and have their work published on the mainland and in other parts of the Chinese-speaking world. This spiritual *haigui*, in my opinion, is also *ban haigui*. By extension, nearly all the Chinese writers who migrated overseas in the past decade belong to this category, including Ha Jin (US), Qiu Xiaolong (US), An Chee Min (US), Shan Sa (France) and Cheng Baoyi (France), perhaps with the exception of Gao Xingjian, the Nobel Prize winner, who vehemently denied any connection with China by saying he has 'nothing to do with that country at all'.[30] I say this because their work represents a spiritual return to the Motherland in their use of Chinese resources and their overwhelming concern for things Chinese, although I critique them as cultural cooks catering to the Western taste.[31]

Ban haigui can be a positive thing, as shown by some artists from Australia, such as Julian Yu, the Australian-Chinese composer who recently toured China with the Melbourne Symphony Orchestra showcasing his musical compositions; Du Jigang, the Melbourne-based Australian-Chinese opera singer, who sings in China and Australia; as well as artist Guan Wei, who is going to exhibit in China late this year. Their links between the East and the West can only be enriching to both.

Writers and artists apart, other intellectuals I know in Australia also belong to this category of *ban haigui* in that they are culturally connected to China through television or the Internet and are kept apart from where they live. In the celebration of the Year of the Sheep, I noticed that many spent the Chinese New Year's Eve watching the *Big Show* on television received from the satellite dish, although my subscription to Foxtel gave me no access to it. With instant access to things Chinese on TV, they seem to be living in an enclave: China inside and Australia outside as soon as the door is closed behind them.

Perhaps the most symbolic act of *ban haigui*, a process of severing and connecting, was done by artist Sheng Qi, now based in Beijing, when he cut off his little finger and buried it in a flowerpot in Beijing before leaving for Rome and London more than a decade ago. He said, 'The process of severing a part of my hand will stay with me through my whole life',[32] because, as one critic says, 'although his body drifted abroad, a part of him, his soul, was still deeply rooted in China'.[33]

Bu haigui

Bu is 'no' and *bu haigui* means refusing to return to China. In my recently published novel, *The Eastern Slope Chronicle*, characters are stuck in a state of betweenness, some trying to *haigui* and failing, others altogether *bu haigui*.[34] Interestingly, one group of people who *bu haigui* is children of the *haiguipai*, born and brought up overseas but having to follow their *haiguipai* parents back to China reluctantly, as they find it harder to adapt to the Chinese situation. Used to the Western *laissez-faire* educational system, many children find the Chinese one harsh and inhumane. For example, they are not allowed to move their hands and legs freely in class, are given too much homework to do, are frightened by their teachers' scolding of other classmates,[35] are criticised for being unable to speak fluent Chinese, are not allowed to run around on the school lawn as it is expensive to maintain the grass, and they do not have Chinese children for friends because of cultural differences. They end up living an isolated life at home, keeping contact with their friends back in the US or Canada and wanting to go back.[36] As a result, some parents have to return to their adopted countries and others are prevented from *haigui* by their children who strongly object to their return.[37]

One 10-year-old said to his parents, 'You two can go back but I won't. I can live here by myself and I can heat my rice with the microwave.' Another boy said, 'Dad, as long as I don't have to go back to China, I shall study hard here and listen to you, including learning Chinese and playing piano [as he hates these last two]'.

And, of course, there are others who cannot go back to China or will not go no matter what and this does not get reported because it is the dark side of the moon. Not long ago, I met some erstwhile political dissidents who came before and after the Tiananmen incident. They, I might say, are still sort of *ban haigui* because they are dealing in business related to China although their applications for visas were constantly rejected by the consulate in Melbourne because their names were on the black list. For the foreseeable future, they will not be able to get out of this limbo, condemned to living a life of dualities.

A recent party at a friend's house in Melbourne reminded me of another reality I had almost forgotten. My friend came to Australia about 15 years ago but when I asked whether he had gone back to China, he said no. Why? He said there was no need as all his family members had gone overseas. He then insinuated that the services in China were not up to standard. I recalled, belatedly, that I had met a number of people like him who claimed that there was no urge for them to go back at all and I happened to know that most of these people were not doing very well, some were on Centrelink payments and others were suffering from work-related injuries, their stories not documented either in Australia or in China. Even those who went back in the mid-1990s came back to Australia without much success, their relationships broken down. Large numbers of cases involving domestic violence and divorce in 1996 and 1997 in Melbourne, for example, attest to this new crisis.

End of the story

Recently, I have watched a number of television dramas made in China and noticed one intriguing phenomenon. In most of them, related to corruption and drug-smuggling or business adventures, Chinese mainlanders and *haiguipai* play good guys and bad guys but the *haiguipai* are invariably portrayed as bad guys, such as the drug-producer, Cong Ke, who returns from his studies in Japan in *shenghuoxiu* (*Life Show*),[38] and Yang Chun, the murderer from America in *heibing* (*Black Ice*).[39] I suspect that is a subtle refraction of a hidden resentment and jealousy towards the *haiguipai*, who, among ordinary people in China, seem to have it both ways: enjoying a safe exit overseas and reaping the benefits of the recent economic boom and government favouritism. As one commentator says, against the *haiguipai*, there is also a *bentupai* (native group) or even *tubie*,[40] who are given only half the benefits to enjoy, and are thus unfairly treated.[41] Another points out that some *haiguipai* return to China because they have to as they are not quite successful overseas and then the halo around their head disappears after a while when they fall far short of expectations.[42] Some even blame the *haiguipai* for causing the Internet melt-down and the plunge in the stockmarket, calling them *haigui* (sea turtles),[43] a homonym for *haigui*.

But, of course, there is another group of people who are currently streaming out of China into private schools in Australia and other countries, supported by their rich or *nouveau riche* parents, but that will be a topic for a separate paper.

In any case, *haigui* as a keyword for 2003 is inevitable as China has entered into the 21st century and the WTO, becoming stronger each year, economically if not politically. In fact, control of the Internet in China reached its peak on 15 January, 2003, when all the poetry web sites (108 of them) were shut down because of the discovery of *Falungong*-related news posted online.[44] One Chinese source based in the US quoted the *New York Times* as saying that China had 'the worst Internet censorship in the world'.[45] It would be interesting to see whether these *haiguipai* attracted by the economic freedom in China will continue to stay despite the political non-freedom.

On my recent visit to San Francisco, I met a Chinese grocery store owner in Chinatown. I asked him where I could find an Internet café, having failed to find any there. He said he did not know as he was too busy minding his shop, working more than 12 hours a day. Then he said to me, obviously taking me for a mainlander, 'America is no good. When you go back, tell them not to come to America.'

'But why did you come? And why did you not return?' I said.

'I'd very much love to return but my children are too small', the man said.

Footnotes

1. Sun Quan. *The Third Wave of Chinese Return: 'China has truly changed!'*. See http://community.tigtag.com/community/overseas/12503_7_6.html《第三次海外华人回归潮"中国真的变了！"》(Please note that all the titles in English of the Chinese articles throughout the footnotes and quotations in the main text are Ouyang's translations.)

2. See Wang Gan. *Winning Men's Eyeballs: Why Do Women Write?*, at http://www.poemlife.com.cn/forum/SoulView.jsp?forumID=16&msgID=2147480156&page=1《赢得男人的眼球：女人为什么写作》

3. *Haigui* in China has reached 140,000. http://www.ccw.com.cn/htm/work/News/02_8_15_5.asp 《中国"海归"达14万 创办企业近4千家》

4. Beijing opened its gate wide for talented people in 23 categories. *Beijing Entertainment Mail*, 15 January, 2003. http://edu.sina.com.cn/l/2003-01-15/36760.html

5. Return waves continue to heat up: *haigui* reaching 32,000 in Shanghai. *Evening News*. 15 January, 2003. http://edu.sina.com.cn/a/2003-01-15/36773.html

6. Attraction for talented people not as good as before? Shenzhen still one of the first choices for *haigui*. *South Metropolitan Daily*, 7 January, 2003. http://news.sina.com.cn/c/2003-01-07/1702865468.shtml

7. See the story on EWS at http://www.gd.xinhua.org/ztbd/ljh/ 24 January, 2003.

8. Students in the United States of America return practice with greater money prospect and *haigui* becoming a wave. *China News Net*, 10 January, 2003. http://edu.sina.com.cn/a/2003-01 10/36584.html

9. Ibid.

10. Ibid.

11. How do state enterprises keep *haigui* talents? 23 January, 2003. http://chanye.sina.net/cs/2003-01-23/134417.shtml#b835122

12. *Haigui* in China has reached 140,000. http://tech.sh.sina.com.cn/it/m/2002-08-14/1658132340.shtml 《中国"海归"达14万创办企业近4千家》

13. Universities in Beijing are vying with each other to engage *haigui* professors. 31 December, 2002. http://www.china.org.cn/chinese/EDU-c/254980.htm 《北京高校争聘"海归"教授》

14. Why Don't Scholars Working Overseas Come Back? http://edu.sina.com.cn/en/2002-12-23/8134.html

15. See Wang Gan, *Winning Men's Eyeballs: Why Do Women Write?*

16   Lin Mohan and Wei Wei (eds). 1999. *We spit on that kind of Chinese: 'Elitists' of the Unrest Overseas.* pp.81–2. Gansu People's Publishing House.
17   In Chinese, *bentu*, literally 'this land', means one's native country. — Ouyang's note.
18   In Chinese, *jiegui*, literally 'aligning the rails with', means to align with. — Ouyang's note.
19   See Wang Gan at http://learning.sohu.com/46/77/article 200847746.shtml
20   See Hong Ying at http://learning.sohu.com/46/77/article 200847746.shtml
21   Li Xiaojun. 2002. Graduates working in Great Britain are like 'chicken ribs'. *21st Century World Herald.* p.32. No. 28. 9 December, 2002.
22   Ibid., p.32.
23   Ibid., p.32.
24   Barrowclough, Nikki. 1996. Lost in the translation. Interview with Ouyang Yu in 'Good Weekend'. p.45. *Sydney Morning Herald*, July 13, 1996.
25   One source says that Australia tops the list as the most favoured place for studies for people in Shanghai, followed by New Zealand and Britain. Investigative report issued on the status of overseas studies from China. p.55. *The Australian Chinese Age*, 31 January, 2003.
26   See Wang Gan, *Winning Men's Eyeballs: Why Do Women Write?*
27   Ibid.
28   Luo Dayou. Dongfang zhizhu (Oriental Pearl). Quoted in Wang Yuechuan, *Haiwai hanxuejie de houxiandai fanzhimin fansi (Postmodern counter-thoughts on anti-colonialism in the world of the overseas Chinese studies).* http://www.culstudies.com/ zhiminfansi.htm
29   See Bian Ji. Ten great literary phenomenon in 2002. China.Com.Cn. http://www.china.com.cn/chinese/RS/257056.htm #b440968
30   Gao Xingjian. 2000. *Yigeren de shengjing (One Man's Bible).* p.440. Hong Kong: Cosmos Books Ltd. (Translation Ouyang's.)
31   See Ouyang Yu. 2002. Motherland, Otherland: Small Issues. Paper presented at 'Kaihua-jieguo zai Haiwai: An International Conference on the Literatures of the Chinese Diaspora', San Francisco, California, 28 November to 1 December, 2002.

32 Huang Du. 2000. Special Focus on Sheng Qi: Sheng Qi's Body and Discourse. *Contemporary Chinese-art.com*. Vol. 3. Issue 2.
33 Ibid.
34 Ouyang Yu. 2002. *The Eastern Slope Chronicle*. Sydney: Brandl & Schlesinger.
35 Xiaohaigui haipa guonei laoshi (Small *haigui* are frightened of teachers in China). 22 August, 2002. The web address for this article, 《"小海归"害怕国内老师》, is no longer in existence, suggesting the article has been removed from the Internet.
36 Embarrassing situation encountered by *haiguipai* children. The web address for this article, 《海歸派子女教育遭遇尷尬》, is no longer in existence, suggesting the article has been removed from the Internet.
37 Cruel reality: children being the greatest pain of *haigui*. *Youth Time News*, 16 January, 2003. http://edu.sina.com.cn/a/2003-01-16/36820.html 《残酷的现实－孩子是"海归"最大的痛》
38 Ibid.
39 Ibid.
40 Ibid.
41 See http://news.xinhuanet.com/ent/2002-10/18/content_601046.htm, based on the novel by Chi Li bearing the same title.
42 See http://www.ahtv.com.cn/gb/content/2001-10/29/content_12305.htm
43 *Tubie*, earth turtles or freshwater turtles, a pejorative term for China-educated intellectuals as opposed to the foreign-educated *haigui*, sea turtles. Successful *haigui* people give a piece of their minds. 17 January, 2003. The web address for this article, 《成功海龟人士谈心得》, is no longer in existence, suggesting the article has been removed from the Internet.
44 Hui Feng. Let *haiguipai* and *bentupai* go to hell. The web address for this article, 《讓海歸派本土派見鬼去吧》, is no longer in existence, suggesting the article has been removed from the Internet.
45 Qiu Wei. Let *haigui* disappear. D:\My Document\Other People's Writing\让"海归"消失.htm
46 Wei Cheng. Seeing through China: talking about the ups and downs of *haiguipai*. The web address for this article, 《透視中國:海歸派沉浮談》, is no longer in existence, suggesting the article has been removed from the Internet.
47 See the notice from Shanghai City Bureau of Telecommunications at http://xxx.clubhi.com/, 16 January, 2003.
48 See the *Netnews at New Threads*. No. 108. January 2003. http://xys.org/xys/magazine/GB/2003/xys0301.txt

5. MURAKAMI HARUKI'S *SYDNEY DIARY*

Leith Morton

This paper will focus on a single volume by acclaimed Japanese author Murakami Haruki (for the purposes of this paper, I will adopt Japanese name order, with surname first) and his *Shidonii!* (*Sydney!*), published in January 2001 by the Bungei Shunjû company in Tokyo. Three-quarters of this 409-page book consists of Murakami's *Shidonii Nisshi* (*Sydney Diary*), which records in 23 daily entries the minutiae of his life in Sydney and his observations of the Sydney Olympics. The book also contains many reflections on Australia and its life and culture.

Murakami is the most popular writer of serious fiction in Japan, having broken the magic four million sales barrier for his 1987 hard-cover novel *Noruwei no Mori* (*Norwegian Wood*). This record still stands in Japan. (Incidentally, despite having been translated into English soon after publication, only last year a new, different English translation of this novel appeared.) So it is safe to say that Murakami's *Sydney Diary* will be read by a very large number of Japanese readers, as all of his books have been. If anyone is capable of 'creating' for Japanese the image of Australia in the 21st century, that person is Murakami.

Before embarking upon a discussion of his *Sydney Diary*, I will briefly sketch an outline of Murakami's career to date.

He was born in Kyoto in 1949 and grew up in the salubrious surroundings of seaside Kobe. He went to Tokyo for his degree and graduated from the literature and theatre school of Waseda University in 1975. His graduation thesis was on the journey motif in American cinema. Murakami was an American specialist and, even after becoming a full-time writer in 1981, he continued a career as a translator of some of the greatest modern American writers into Japanese. His translations include works by F. Scott Fitzgerald, Truman Capote, Raymond Carver, John Irving and Tim O'Brien.

Murakami has won most of the major Japanese literary awards. His best-known novels include the trilogy *1979 Nen no Pinbōru* (*1979. Pinball*, 1980), *Hitsuji o Meguru Bōken* (*A Wild Sheep Chase*, 1982) and *Dansu Dansu Dansu* (*Dance, Dance, Dance*, 1988). He has also written much non-fiction, including his well-known study of the Sarin gas attack by the Aum terrorist group on the Tokyo subways, *Undāguraundo* (*Underground*, 1997). All of his major novels — which have now sold into double figures — and some of his non-fiction have been translated into English. Already two books in English have been written on Murakami and, no doubt, there will be many more. He has lived overseas for long periods — mostly in Europe and the US — often in an attempt to escape media attention. One important fact to keep in mind for the purposes of this paper is Murakami's excellent reading and speaking skills in English.

Passing, fugitive references to Australia occur in some of his fiction, rather like distinguished French novelist George Perec's (1936–82) use of Australian names in his writing, and Umberto Eco's famous essay on the platypus. That is, Australia is a source of exotica, so the odd kangaroo bounding through Murakami's fiction simply reminds us that for most non-Australian intellectuals, Australia represents a mythic land of exotic beasts located at the end of the Earth. As far as I am aware, the visit to the Olympics was Murakami's first trip to Australia.

Murakami has, however, written on the Olympic Games before: in 1987, he published a volume called *The Scrap — The*

Good Old 1980s in which he constructed a portrait of the US during the '80s by combing American magazines and newspapers from the era for interesting stories. He comments in the form of a diary on the 1984 Los Angeles Olympics. Murakami has also written travelogues before. In 1990 and 1991 he published, first, a book on his three-year residence in Europe from 1986 to 1989, and, second, a book on his travels in Greece and Turkey. In addition, in 1998, he published a volume entitled *Henkyō Kinkyō* (*Borders Near and Far*) containing essays on his travels in the US, Mexico and Inner Mongolia, where he visited Nomonhan — the site of a famous battle between the Soviet Union and Japan in 1939. This event forms the centrepiece of his 1994 mega novel, originally published in four volumes in Japanese, *Nejimaki Tori Kuronikuru* (*The Wind-Up Bird Chronicle*). So Murakami did not come to the Sydney Olympics without significant experience of writing travel literature and an Olympic diary.

As he notes in his postscript to the volume, however, his *Sydney Diary* was the first time he had written so much in such a short time. At several places in the text he tells us that he is typing his reportage of a specific event on his laptop at the venue while the event is taking place. As Murakami puts it, this is 'real-time' writing, although not all of the diary entries are composed in this way. Most were written at night in his hotel after the day's events were concluded. Also, it is important to note that it is a real diary — he records what he had for breakfast on each of the 23 days of his diary, how much it cost, what the weather was like while he was jogging or bike-riding around the Sydney Opera House and Botanical Gardens (his regular morning route), how long it took him to complete the circuit and what clothes he wore on the day. Thus, the diary is an intensely personal document, and Murakami's diary persona (which bears a strong resemblance to the eponymous hero — simply called '*boku*' or 'I' — who appears in many of his fictional narratives) becomes the reader's friend.

This paper concentrates on the picture of Australia that Murakami draws, not on the text as a whole, which deserves at least another paper. If I was to write such a paper, my interest would focus on the text and, in particular, its narrative structure, as a species of 'life-writing' or 'autobiographical fiction', a genre which has become one of the dominant modes of late 20th-century writing. There is no doubt that the intimate, frank portrait of Murakami painted in this book presents a compelling subject for readers, and projects a reader who can get to know this most famous of contemporary Japanese authors on a personal, intimate level. But such analysis is better left for another day.

In the book itself, Murakami makes a few passing references to his fame: the interview with the literary columnist of the *Australian*, an interview with a Korean TV journalist, the way in which the journal and the publisher sponsoring and paying for Murakami's visit respond to his every need immediately. Tickets that can be bought only from scalpers for exorbitant prices for events such as the opening and closing ceremonies and the 400-metres final involving Cathy Freeman, are all obtained for Murakami instantly. His expensive laptop is replaced by his benefactor the day after it is stolen from his Sydney hotel room. His benefactor, or should we say 'minder', is employed by the publisher. However, all these references are made openly — Murakami is staggered by the munificence of his sponsors — or so it is made to appear — he can't believe how much these tickets cost.

Murakami repeatedly tells us how much he dislikes the Olympics, and how appallingly boring most of the events are. At one point, he writes the word '*taikutsu*' (boring) several times in the one sentence in case we haven't got the idea. Naturally, this criticism of the Olympics is balanced by mention of the strange paradox that it is, nevertheless, astonishingly compelling, and Murakami has no regrets whatever about being despatched all the way from Japan to the end of the world to report on the event.

So we are given to understand as readers that this is one man's, one writer's, view of the Sydney Olympics and Australia in general: Murakami revels in his own idiosyncracies. Several times he notes, dear reader, you may well have a completely different view of the Olympics from your TV viewing, and your view may be the correct one. My opinion is that while this kind of rhetoric may protect Murakami against criticism of his reporting as subjective rather than objective, the real motive for it lies in the creation of a cantankerous, maverick friend called Murakami who is so intimate with his readers that he will disclose to us exactly what he really thinks, just as a close friend should. In other words, it is a rhetorical strategy (probably a perfectly sincere one) designed to create a special kind of relationship between author and reader, one which goes far beyond mere journalism.

Let us now examine specific segments of the text to ascertain exactly how Murakami 'creates' Australia for his Japanese audience, and what kind of Australia he has created. I should note before commencing this analysis that the bulk of the diary entries are concerned overwhelmingly with meticulous descriptions of various Olympic events in which Murakami is interested — especially the men's and women's marathon. Only three or four diary entries out of the 23 concentrate on Australian life and culture; other observations on Australia emerge just in passing.

Also, I will mostly exclude the numerous mentions of Australian flora and fauna that Murakami seeks in koala parks, zoos and museums, preferring to emphasise instead his analysis of Australian history and society. It is worth noting, however, that there are a number of two- or three-page digressions on topics of particular interest — koalas, sharks, shark attacks, poisonous snakes and spiders, bushfires — which usually incorporate much detailed information gleaned from various reference works on Australian mammals, reptiles and so on. This information appears to derive from various reference works by authors such as Eric Rolls, Gerry Swan and Terence Lindsay purchased at bookshops and museums (which are listed in the bibliography).

Like the early European explorers of Australia — whose accounts Murakami has read in Tim Flannery's 1998 volume

The Explorers, which he cites now and again — Murakami comments several times on how strange and weird the Australian landscape is. The view from the aeroplane flying over the vast deserts of Australia is, he says, 'like a Tim Burton movie'; he is transported to another dimension (p.50).[1] He notes that Australia is the hottest, driest continent and recounts the migration in antiquity of marsupials and Aborigines from other land masses to this sunburnt country (p.51). The western suburbs of Sydney, however, are less romantic; the view from a train trip before the games begin reveals a crumbling, faded cityscape (p.62). This comment comes from the entry for 12 September, when Murakami journeyed to Parramatta to see the Olympic flame relay.

The didactic design of the novelist can be seen in his mini-history of Parramatta from its first Aboriginal settlement through colonial times to the present. Clearly, Murakami is intending to educate his audience about Australia. He also lets us know that 'strine' puzzled him at first but his ears quickly make the adjustment and, for the rest of his stay, he has no trouble understanding Australian English, although he discusses its peculiarities from time to time, notably the habit of abbreviating everything: salt-water crocodiles, he writes, are called 'salties' (pp.60–73).

Murakami's analysis of the symbolism of the opening ceremony on 15 September is insightful. He sees the panorama as an attempt to promote a post-reconciliation brand of patriotism — to do away with memories of the convict past and the dispossession of Aboriginal lands by white settlers. These observations follow a mini-history of Homebush (the site of the Olympics), in which Murakami outlines the history of white exploitation of Aborigines. For him, such a politically correct version of patriotism is tendentious but also rather countrified. His comment on the theatre of the opening ceremony is that it is a load of 'bucolic mummery' (pp.95–100), although he later admits that the architectural excellence of the main stadium surprised him, saying there is nothing as sophisticated as this in Japan.

On 19–20 September, he drives up the coast to Brisbane in a Ford Falcon with a friend to see Japan play Brazil in a preliminary soccer match. He is staggered by the vastness of the territory — and a massive bushfire he encounters on the way. A country cop who pulls him over for speeding is proud of this bushfire, which has been burning for a week. Apart from his shock at how law-abiding Australian motorists are — Japanese drivers always speed on highways, and no one cares, he says — he is intrigued by the Australian attitude towards bushfires. After enjoying the luxury of a five-star hotel in Brisbane, he journeys to the soccer match. The stadium is full of young Japanese waving Rising-Sun flags. Murakami reflects that, although this is uncontroversial now, how many of the same Japanese youth would be aware of the Japanese bombing of Darwin in World War II, and the casualties that resulted (pp.146–177)?

Apart from the casual mention of Australian novels he is reading, such as Patrick White's *Voss* and Peter Carey's *True History of the Kelly Gang*, it is clear that Murakami gains most of his information from newspapers. As part of his morning routine, he trots to the nearby convenience store to buy copies of the local papers — The *Australian*, *Sydney Morning Herald* and the *Daily Telegraph* — which he reads from cover to cover, and cuts out articles of interest to peruse further at night. He frequently quotes from the papers — summarising their daily content for his readers. One topic that he mentions several times in the lead-up to Cathy Freeman's victory in the 400-metres final on 25 September is the hate mail she attracts from newspaper readers who object to her lighting the Olympic torch or, after her win, brandishing the Aboriginal flag. In his entry for 26 September, he analyses the pressure on her and disagrees with criticisms of her assertion of Aboriginality.

The most detailed analysis of Australia in his book comes with the 13-page entry on 28 September in which Murakami styles a short history of Australia — from the First Fleet to the Olympics — from the perspective of a disturbed individual, that is, Murakami. For this entry, he obviously drew upon Flannery's research as well as Geoffrey Blainey's *Short History of Australia*, which is cited in its original edition and the Japanese translation. He notes that half of the convicts on the First Fleet committed serious crimes — they were not all Fenian rebels. But the fact of Australia being founded as a penal colony determined its destiny; this was in contrast to the US. The American rebels deliberately broke their ties with Britain to pursue their separate dreams.

Australia — here Murakami uses the metaphor Mother England and her faithful child — and, especially its ruling class, tried to win its mother's affection by volunteering to fight in war after war which had no connection with Australia: the Sudan conflict, the Boer War, World War I and so on. He describes the huge Australian losses in the Gallipoli campaign as a sacrifice to erase the convict stain. But when Britain sent its forces to Europe to fight Hitler, and thus abandoned Australia, Australia was forced to turn to its elder brother, the US, for help. In the postwar era, Australia became America's deputy sheriff in the region. For Murakami, this clinging to other nations for security reveals Australia's anxiety over its identity, its failure to articulate its own sense of destiny (pp.273–281).

From Australia's participation in the Vietnam War, however, and the strong opposition to the conflict that emerged at the time, a new sense of identity was born. Murakami links this to the birth of the multicultural ideal in Australia. Returning to his Freudian metaphor, he argues Australia conquered its childish separation trauma and grew up to develop mature relations with its Asian neighbours. The one remaining thorn under the skin of Australian identity was the question of Aborigines. Murakami notes that they were not counted in the census as citizens until the 1960s. Australia's attempts to impose its own standards of human rights on its Asian neighbours failed because of this blatant hypocrisy, he argues. Once Australia moved towards reconciliation and celebrated National Sorry Day, then, in this respect as well, Australia began to mature as a nation. This leads him to Cathy Freeman.

Her maternal grandmother was a victim of the Stolen Generation. At the root of this policy, Murakami discerns an economic motive. The politics of racial separation were designed to create a cheap serf caste of Aboriginal labourers and stockmen. He discusses the failure of High Court cases to recompense Aborigines for their suffering arising out of being forcibly separated from their parents. Murakami describes the verdict of the Supreme Court of NSW in the Joy Williams case as a 'political judgment'. He asserts that the pain and suffering endured by Freeman's grandmother as a result of her forced separation from her mother affected Cathy's entire family, and this same pain resides deep in Cathy's heart (pp.281–284).

The source of this information was an interview Freeman gave to an English newspaper earlier in 2000. So Murakami views Cathy's tears at the 400-metres awards ceremony (noting that she hardly expressed any emotion prior to this) as emblematic of reconciliation. The tears in the eyes of the Australians in the stadium watching the ceremony he interprets as a sharing of her pain. Cathy Freeman, he wrote, is a kind of female shaman enduring catharsis for the sake of the nation. Murakami himself was deeply affected by this and wept as well — in this sense, the Sydney Olympics is a spiritual turning point, a milestone in the history of Australia (p.284).

The only other entry in which Murakami offers a sustained analysis of Australian society is towards the end of his three-week sojourn in the country. In the entry for 2 October, he observes that Australians love a party and, as the quality of their food is superior to the US and Britain (and cheaper), why not? This leads Murakami to an analysis of Australia as a quarry to the world (with Japan as its biggest customer). The fact that, historically, Australia is a mineral treasure trove has led to the easygoing, relaxed mode of Australian life — it gave rise to the idea of the lucky country.

But, writes Murakami, with the sophisticated mining technology now available, Third-World countries can export mineral resources to Asia more cheaply than Australia, thus Australia's resource-export dependent macro-economy is in a long-term decline. This is now becoming apparent in the growing trade deficit. Murakami fears Australia's happy-go-lucky character will inevitably change — the Olympics brightened the gloom for a tiny moment (pp.331–345).

My reading of Murakami's observations is that, given that he was in the country for only three weeks, his opinions are better informed than most, and better expressed than often is the case for the few Japanese intellectuals who have written about Australia. In fact, his professionalism shines through — doing so much research in just three weeks, even if it was mostly scrutinising the daily newspapers with a fine-tooth comb. Perhaps his take on Cathy Freeman as a spiritual medium, symbolising in her victory the triumph of reconciliation, is a tad too romantic but, on the other hand, Murakami might respond that you had to be there in the stadium at that moment. The poetic power of the novelist's fine prose style is revealed here to good effect, and it is, after all, the artist who is our contemporary myth-maker, and thus the custodian of the future.

Murakami's mixed prose style, which varies tenses and register according to the entry, discloses how his diary was composed: sometimes while he was watching an event and sometimes later. It also creates a marvellous sense of verisimilitude which further acts to strengthen the sympathetic persona of the author: a harried, harassed journalist doing his best for his readers. It is noticeable that Murakami was accredited as a journalist for the games, and had the wide access granted to journalists. He reminds us at the end of his book of one of his cultural heroes, Ernest Hemingway, who also wrote as a journalist on the Spanish Civil War. *For Whom the Bell Tolls* arose out of that experience; I wonder whether Murakami will turn his novelistic skills to a similar end.

One final observation I will make is just how important Murakami's near-native ability in English was to his account. Not many Australians read three daily newspapers cover to cover every morning before they go to work. Murakami's easy grasp of the avalanche of information pouring out of the

Olympic machine, television, newspapers and radio (I should mention that I'm sure that at one point John Laws is the middle-aged Australian speaking on talk-back who he listens to on a taxi radio) made his task easier than has been for other Japanese writers I have read, who compose the occasional essay after visiting Australia full of egregious errors that could have been corrected by reading the daily newspaper.

In general, his generation of Japanese intellectuals has a better command of English than some earlier generations, although not many are as expert as Murakami. This, I think, was a major factor in his construction of Australia — for it is an Australia that I, for one, have no trouble recognising, and in fact find that, for the most part, it is a vision of Australia, with all its flaws and virtues, that I might well embrace.

Footnote

[1] All page references are to the edition of *Sydney!* mentioned in the text.

6. TAMPA IN JAPAN

EAST ASIAN RESPONSES TO AUSTRALIA'S REFUGEE POLICY

Tessa Morris-Suzuki

In the past few years Australia has experienced the slow death of a long-cherished myth: the myth that the vicissitudes of domestic political debate have little impact on Australia's image in the Asian region and the wider world. When the debate about Hansonism was at its height, we were repeatedly reassured by political leaders that Pauline Hanson's unfortunate public statements created no more than passing ripples in the calm seas of our relations with Asia. More recently, government ministers have insisted that Australia's firm line on asylum-seekers is doing no lasting harm to the country's international reputation. Indeed, Philip Ruddock has informed us that Australia's migration procedures are recognised world-wide as best practice, and that other countries are eagerly following Australia's lead.[1] On this occasion, though, sceptics in the media and opposition parties have repeatedly voiced their concerns about the direction in which Australia is heading, and the damage current policy is causing to Australia's image as a tolerant and multicultural society.

Here I shall consider responses in Japan to Australia's asylum-seeker policy, focusing particularly on Japanese media reports on the 2001 *'Tampa* crisis'. This extends work by others who have looked at reporting of the incident in South-East Asia and elsewhere. From a survey of three English-language newspapers in Singapore, Malaysia and Indonesia, for example, Denise Woods has suggested that the incident reinforced, rather than negatively altered, Australia's image in South-East Asia.[2] My argument here is that the incident did indeed have a negative effect on the way in which a considerable number of people in Japan view Australia. But I shall also suggest that it is worth paying attention to Japanese media accounts of the *Tampa* incident, not simply because they cast light on the way in which 'they' see 'us', but for more profound and complex reasons. Among other things, they raise questions about the boundaries of 'domestic affairs', and indeed about the very boundaries between 'us' and 'them', in the 21st-century world.

This paper does not attempt to survey the whole gamut of Japanese reporting on the *Tampa* incident, but instead focuses on the print media. I begin by looking at newspaper reports of the incident and then go on to look in rather more detail at one particularly interesting magazine article on the issue.

Boatpeople, illegal migrants, refugees: Japanese newspapers and the *Tampa* crisis

The comfortable hypothesis that Australia's asylum policy is likely to make little impact on our image in Asia seems to rest on three propositions. The first is that (at least as far as China and Japan are concerned) Australia attracts very little media attention, and few reporters are likely to have paid much attention to such remote issues as *Tampa* and the so-called 'Pacific Solution'. The second is that other countries in the region, including Japan, have poor records in relation to refugees and therefore (to put it smugly) 'they' have no grounds for criticising 'us'. Thirdly, by extension, most governments in the region today are much more concerned with developing methods to keep out 'illegal immigrants' than with protecting the rights of asylum-seekers, and are therefore more likely to respond with sympathy than with disapproval to Australia's stance.

All of these propositions contain at least a grain of truth. The *Tampa* crisis was never headline news in Japan (as it was in some European countries). Most Japanese people are unlikely to have heard of the *Tampa*, and most of those who have some hazy memory of the incident are unlikely to remember the details. The Japanese Government has shown itself extraordinarily unresponsive to recent refugee crises, detaining and refusing refugee status to the only nine Afghans to seek asylum in Japan to escape persecution by the Taliban. In November 2001 the Tokyo District Court ruled that five of these asylum-seekers were to be released on the grounds that detaining potential refugees simply on suspicion that they were illegal immigrants contravened the Convention on Refugees, but the Justice Ministry promptly appealed the decision, which was reversed the next month. Thereupon the asylum-seekers were immediately re-arrested and returned to incarceration in the Eastern Japan detention centre in Ushiku City.[3] In the circumstances, it is not surprising that, at the summit meeting between Prime Ministers Howard and Koizumi in the first half of 2002, one of the key items on the agenda was cooperation to deal with the 'transnational crime' of people smuggling. In this sense, Philip Ruddock may well be right to highlight the 'general acknowledgment overseas' of Australia's 'expertise' in keeping out the unwanted.

On the other hand, the *Tampa* incident perhaps attracted more media attention than any other recent event in Australia after the Olympics. Between 28 August, 2001, when the first reports appeared, and 11 September, when *Tampa* was driven off the pages of the newspapers by other more momentous events, Japan's national and major regional daily newspapers ran 50 articles on the issue (see Table 1).[4] By comparison, the rise of Pauline Hanson (which was also widely reported in Japan) generated just 17 articles in the whole of 1996, and, from

28 August to 11 October, 2001, when the final analysis of the results appeared, there were just seven reports on the 2001 Australian Federal Election.

Table 1. Japanese newspaper reports on the *Tampa* crisis, 28 August–11 September, 2001

Newspaper	No. of Reports
Asahi	10
Yomiuri	8
Mainichi	7
Nikkei	5
Sankei	3
Regional Papers	17
Total	**50**

Like most Japanese news reports, the articles on the *Tampa* crisis were relatively bland in tone and seldom included overt expressions of opinion. Many were also very short. Yet at the same time they offer some interesting glimpses of the concerns which the issue raised in various sections of Japanese opinion. When the first reports appeared in the major dailies on 28 and 29 August, journalists and editors seemed uncertain about how to frame this story. Several newspapers described the people picked up by the Norwegian cargo ship *Tampa* as 'boatpeople' (*bōtopīpuru*), and most seemed to rely mainly on Australian official sources for their information. For example, the *Asahi* newspaper, in a short article published on 28 August, reported that survivors from a sinking boat had been picked up two days earlier by a Norwegian freighter, the *Tampa*, between Java and Christmas Island, and that the rescued 'boatpeople' had forcibly insisted that the captain head for Australian waters. 'However, on the same day, the Australian government refused the *Tampa* entry into its territorial waters on the grounds that "under international law this problem should be resolved between Indonesia and Norway" [Prime Minister Howard]'.[5] Other papers also reported Howard's words, although the *Mainichi* also quoted a statement by the

Norwegian Foreign Minister to the effect that, as the nearest country, Australia had a duty to allow the rescued asylum-seekers to come on shore.[6]

As the crisis unfolded, however, coverage of the issue in the various newspapers began to take on subtly different nuances. One indicator of difference was the use of words. After the initial reports, three of the major dailies (the *Asahi*, *Mainichi* and *Yomiuri*) generally adopted the practice of referring to the *Tampa* asylum-seekers as 'refugees' (*nanmin*), while the right-of-centre *Sankei* newspaper and the business-oriented *Nihon Keizai* newspaper, commonly abbreviated to *Nikkei*, usually referred to them as 'illegal migrants' (*mikkōsha*).

Indeed, the *Sankei* and *Nikkei* appeared relatively sympathetic to the Australian Government's position. In its initial account of the crisis, the *Sankei* reported that 'the freighter [*Tampa*] endeavoured to take the boatpeople to the nearest Indonesian port, but several of them seem to have become agitated and burst on to the bridge, forcing the ship to steer towards the Australian territory of Christmas Island. The Australian government insists that "it is the international rule that people who are rescued at sea should be taken to the nearest port". The authorities have already faced problems, since more than 1,300 refugees have arrived at Christmas Island in the past two weeks'.[7] The *Nikkei* similarly concluded its first brief report of the incident with the words, 'The number of illegal migrants trying to reach Australia via Indonesia and other countries has grown suddenly in recent years. This year alone 3,800 illegal migrants have been found'.[8]

In fuller reports, which appeared three days later, the *Sankei* and *Nikkei* gave prominence to José Ramos Horta's suggestion that East Timor might be willing to provide refuge to some of the asylum-seekers — the *Sankei* interpreting this as an act of 'gratitude' (*ongaeshi*) for Australia's past assistance to East Timorese refugees — though both papers also noted the 'rising international criticism' of Australia over the crisis.[9]

In the other daily papers, by contrast, implicit criticism of Australia's stance was much more apparent. The right-of-centre *Yomiuri*, also reporting Ramos Horta's proposal, preceded this by outlining the proposal from the United Nations High Commission for Refugees (UNHCR) that Australia should allow the *Tampa* asylum-seekers to disembark on Christmas Island for processing, and that Indonesia, Australia and Norway should be jointly responsible for accepting those found to have a legitimate claim to be refugees.[10] This UNHCR proposal was particularly widely reported in Japan, appearing not just in articles in the national *Yomiuri* and *Mainichi* newspapers, but in regional papers.[11]

On 5 September, when it was clear that Australia was not going to accept this proposal, the *Yomiuri* returned to the topic with a note of sharper criticism, emphasising the 'unconcealed disappointment' of Erika Feller, head of the UNHCR's International Protection Bureau (and an Australian former diplomat), that Australia had opted to pursue the 'Pacific Solution' instead of adopting the UNHCR plan, which in Feller's words was 'humane and in accordance with the Refugee Convention'. (It should be noted in passing that the term 'Pacific Solution' is never used in the Japanese newpaper accounts, which refer, less euphemistically, to 'the proposal to move the refugees to New Zealand and Nauru'.) The paper reported Feller's concerns that Australia's refusal to allow the asylum-seekers ashore had created a 'bad precedent' and that the refugees faced an uncertain fate in Nauru, which had a population of just 11,000 and no clearly defined policy on asylum.

At the same time, the newspaper placed the *Tampa* crisis in the context of the global problem of defining refugee status. In particular, it emphasised the growing phenomenon of 'economic refugees' who left their home countries for reasons of poverty rather than for fear of persecution, and noted the need to develop new international norms for classifying and recognising refugees.[12]

The transformation of 'tolerant' Australia
The most detailed coverage of the *Tampa* incident appeared in the middle-of-the-road *Mainichi* newspaper and in the *Asahi*,

generally regarded as the most left-leaning of Japan's national dailies. By 31 August, the *Mainichi* was not only reporting the facts of the unfolding crisis, but beginning to offer some perspective on its context: 'In the past two weeks, some 1,500 boatpeople have arrived in Australia, evoking a strong negative reaction from the Australian people. The [Government's] hardening stance appears to be closely connected to the domestic issue of the forthcoming general election in the latter part of this year'.[13]

Though the *Mainichi* carried just seven articles on the issue, these included relatively lengthy and analytical pieces, not just from the paper's reporters in Australia, but from its European and Central Asian bureaux. On 2 September, for example, the *Mainichi*'s London correspondent reported the refusal of the *Tampa*'s captain to cooperate with the proposed 'Pacific Solution', on the grounds that Australia had not explained how it proposed to move the asylum-seekers to New Zealand and Nauru, and that the *Tampa* lacked the means to transfer them safely from one vessel to another at sea. The reporter also quoted Associated Press reports of the Norwegian embassy's efforts to lodge a claim for refugee status on behalf of the *Tampa* asylum-seekers.[14]

Meanwhile, in a long article made up of reports from correspondents in Islamabad, London and Geneva, the newspaper reflected on the Afghan refugee problem in its wider international context. The outflow of refugees from Afghanistan, it noted, went back to the time of the Soviet invasion. Since then, some two million refugees had fled from Afghanistan to Iran and Pakistan, and recent droughts had further swelled the influx into Pakistan. The article goes on, 'The Afghans and others who were recently rescued by a Norwegian freighter after an Indonesian people-smuggling boat sank were on their way to Australia, which was a popular destination for refugees. It is highly likely that the question of accepting Afghan refugees, who seek to escape their home country by many routes, will become a major problem for the international community'.[15]

The *Asahi* carried the largest number of reports on the crisis and, although many of its articles were quite brief, it picked up aspects of the story overlooked by the other national dailies. On 3 September it noted efforts by a group of Melbourne lawyers to obtain a ruling preventing the 'boatpeople' from being removed from Australian territory.[16] On September 11 it reported that Nauru had agreed to 'accept for refugee processing the 237 boatpeople detained by the Australian navy on 8 [September]. This is in addition to the 280 whom it has already agreed to accept. In repayment, Australia will provide aid to the substantial amount of 2 million Australian dollars [about 12.5 billion yen] in the form of guarantees of diesel fuel, writing off Nauru's debts to Australia for medical programs, etc.'[17] The paper even cited John Howard among its 'quotes of the day' for expressing his anger that people from 'countries which do not accept refugees' had the temerity to criticise his government's inhumanity.[18]

But the paper's most extended reflections on the issue appeared several months after the event, in an article published in January 2002 to mark the 50th anniversary of the Geneva Convention on the Status of Refugees. The article consists of an overview of the state of refugee policy in various parts of the world, beginning with a section entitled 'The Transformation of "Tolerant" Australia'. This notes that events in Afghanistan had generated some 3.6 million refugees, including 'people fleeing persecution, who are protected by the [Geneva] Convention' and 'those "refugees" in the broad sense who are fleeing the disasters of war, etc., but are outside the framework of the Convention'. The article then continues:

> On 26 August last year, in the sea near Australia's Christmas Island, the Norwegian ship Tampa rescued more than 400 Afghan asylum-seekers from a sinking boat and tried to take them to the island. The Australian government refused to let it enter port.
>
> Since abandoning the 'White Australia' policy in the early '70s, Australia had been tolerant of refugees. It accepted almost 200,000 refugees from Indo-China.

Even now it receives roughly 10,000 refugees per year.

This country took a step which, however you look at it, cannot be regarded as humanitarian.

Why has this transformation taken place? The article goes on to outline some of the reasons: Australia, it says, saw itself as being in danger of being swamped by refugees. Many came via South-East Asia after paying large sums of money to 'people smugglers'. 'Last year, in the months to August, 3,694 people had tried to enter the country illegally, and there were repeated arrests and forcible deportations. The government and the people were sick and tired of it. The *Tampa* incident was the outcome of all this. Expecting a tough fight in the up-coming elections, the ruling conservatives took a hard line to win the support of the populace'.[19]

After surveying evidence of hardening attitudes to refugees in other countries, including Britain, France and Germany, the article concludes by arguing the need for new international efforts to address the problems of defining refugees and responding to refugee crises in a changing world. In particular, it returns to the question of so-called 'economic refugees', pointing out that the original notion of asylum built into the Geneva Convention is inadequate to deal with the large numbers of people who seek refuge from genuine suffering — caused, for example, by famine or war — but who do not face a 'threat of persecution' as defined by the convention: 'The time has come when a system created to protect people from oppression must face up to the task of responding to people who seek to flee famine and poverty, as well as war and conflict. Determining how to define "refugees in need of protection" in a humanitarian spirit which maintains fundamental principles is a task that requires the imagination and effort of the international community'.[20]

Viewing the world from the *Tampa*

The *Tampa* crisis, then, attracted considerable attention from the Japanese print media. News reporting of the issue reveals, predictably enough, that there was not one 'Japanese perspective' on the issue, rather various groups within Japan responded in different ways. Beneath the bland and descriptive style which characterises most Japanese newspaper reportage, contesting concerns are evident. For some, the issue was primarily a matter of border controls — the Australian Government was struggling to deal with the problem of 'illegal migrants'. Since Japan also faced similar problems, they were able to express a degree of implicit sympathy for the Howard Government's determination to 'draw the line'.

For others, by contrast, the issue at stake was the humanitarian treatment of refugees, and the refusal of the Australian Government to accept the solution proposed by the UNHCR. The 'transformation of "tolerant" Australia' was an issue of concern to some people in Japan because this image of 'tolerance' had given hope to those who aspired to make their own society more open to migrants and more accepting of its existing diversity. 'Tolerant Australia' could be used as a yardstick with which to measure and criticise existing realities in Japan, and to press for domestic reform. Even after *Tampa*, this use of the Australian 'other' did not entirely disappear, but the language used to evoke the 'other' underwent a telling change. For example, in a searing critique of Japan's refugee policy published in the left-of-centre monthly magazine *Sekai* (*The World*) in July 2002, journalist Isozaki Yumi observed that '*even Australia*, which like Japan has attracted criticism from the international community for its detention and exclusion of refugees' had accepted far more Afghan refugees than Japan (emphasis added).[21]

But it is another article, coincidentally published in the same journal, which offers the most interesting Japanese-language reflections on the *Tampa* crisis. The article takes the form of an interview conducted by the journal's editor-in-chief, Okamoto Atsushi, with Korean academic and writer Lee Chong-Hwa, who has lived and taught in Japan for more than a decade. Lee has published a number of works in Japanese and is best known for her book *Tsubuyaki no seiji shisô* (roughly translatable as *Murmurings of Political Thought*), a work which explores questions of identity, the female body, diversity and political action in an oblique and aphoristic style which often seems as close to poetry as prose.[22] The *Sekai* interview, too, contains wide-reaching reflections on the state of the post-11 September world, drawing on metaphor, memory and personal experience. It is entitled 'Viewing the World from the Refugee Ship *Tampa*'.[23]

Okamoto opens the interview by recalling that Lee spent the year 2001 in London, and asking her about the perspective this had given her on the events of 11 September, the war in Afghanistan and the Palestinian *intifada*. Her response might come as something of a shock to many Australian readers. She replies that her stay in London 'had nothing in particular to do with 11 September, and I do not want to connect the two'. Rather, 'if I were to select one thing, it would be the *Tampa*. The freighter *Tampa* was within me all the time. In the spring of last year I went from Seikei University, where I now work, to London University to conduct overseas research, and in the summer I moved apartments. At just that time, my everyday life became laden with the *Tampa*. If my memory is correct it was a little after 20 August. It seemed that every day the story of the *Tampa* flowed from the radio, and from morning to evening I was together with the *Tampa*. In the midst of all this I felt as though I myself had somehow embarked on this ship *Tampa*'.[24]

In the discussion that follows, the *Tampa* is evoked as a real place of human suffering and as a metaphor for the state of the world. The physical presence of the ship is conjured up with words whose lyricism highlights the ironies of the image. 'I still remember. I think it was 3 September. I opened the *Guardian* newspaper and there, right in front of my eyes, big enough to cover almost half the page, was the most beautiful photograph. It's beautiful, what a lovely photo, I thought. If it hadn't been for the explanation underneath, it would really have been a beautiful photo of the *Tampa*. The *Tampa* is the colour of earth, and is bathed in light, and behind you can see the Australian naval boat coming to attack it. The light is sparkling on the sea and two white seagulls are flying in the sky. Without thinking about it, I cut out this photograph with scissors and stuck it on the white wall of the room into which I had just moved'.[25]

The beauty of this distant scene, of course, conceals the misery of a situation where, as Lee notes, almost 500 people were crammed into a ship designed to accommodate 45, floating in limbo off Christmas Island as the Australian Government demonstrated its refusal to allow this human 'cargo' to touch Australian soil. The reasons for her own absorbtion in the *Tampa* crisis, Lee suggests, lie buried in part in her memories: 'I was born on an island. When I speak of boats I think of seasickness. Whatever else there may be, there is sickness, suffering: from first class to third class — it used to be my dream to travel in first class. Only a few boats had first class cabins. In the third class rooms, which were usually right at the bottom, underneath the bridge — in Korean called the "*kappan*" — I would clutch my stomach and try to endure the sickness, wondering how I could at least get to a place where I could breathe. I remember it vividly. Somehow the people on the *Tampa*, each of them one by one, came to be overlaid on that memory'.[26]

This memory becomes a starting point for considering how we connect with the suffering of others. How, for example, can people in Japan or Europe begin to find a thread of connection that allows them to imagine the experiences of Afghans during the war that expelled the Taliban? The problem, Lee suggests, is not just one of physical distance or different 'cultures', for even South Koreans struggle to imagine and form bonds of empathy with the experience of North Koreans. Ultimately the issue is whether we can draw out, from our own lives, memories that link us to others. 'The reason why I found myself seeing the figures of the people on the *Tampa*, why I cannot forget them is, in a word, the memory of boats. I think the dreadful childhood memory of seasickness has somehow created a physiological connection'.[27]

The problems of memory are made all the more urgent by the state of the world in which we live: a world where dreams are swamped by the obsessive demand for security. After outlining the course of the *Tampa* crisis, Lee observes that, as a result, Prime Minister Howard gained popularity and won the 2001 general election. 'The voices of those demanding safety, security became louder. Asian refugees were undesirable because no one knew what they might do. In circumstances like that, the ideals of diversity and multi-ethnicity, which Australia had held until then, had no power. If we think about it now, in the political moves in Australia surrounding the *Tampa* — the voices of people calling for security, the outcome of the election — we can see in miniature the image of everything that was to follow later'.[28]

'Everything that was to follow later' includes the aftermath of 11 September, when the US intervened in Afghanistan and then turned its attention to Iraq and beyond in its ever-widening 'global war on terror'. Lee likens the US to a sinking ship — a ship carrying millions and generations of migrants and refugees from many countries all over the world. The ship is sinking, but not everything and everybody will sink with it: 'It was the same with the *Tampa* which took on the refugees: if the ship sinks, the nation may be destroyed, but the people still have to live somehow ... So, even if it sinks, how can we can retrieve some things from it — however small and individual and diverse those things may be?'.[29]

With the gradual sinking of this ship, which once symbolised freedom and democracy for so many people around the world, the task of 'retrieving something' becomes a task of memory. More precisely, Lee suggests, what is important is 're-memory', the retrieval of forgotten human connections which may enable us to 're-model' the societies in which we live. 'Re-memory' reveals not only faces and sensations from the past, but the repressed and forgotten faces of the present. For example, Lee notes that among the figures which metaphorically 'appear' on the deck of the *Tampa* are the figures of Korea's Muslims, about whom she had previously known nothing. 'There are, it seems, about 100,000 Muslims on the Korean Peninsula. Of this 100,000, about 30,000 are said to be South Korean. Which means that among the remaining 70,000, many are foreign workers'.[30] The link of empathy with the frightened, seasick passengers on the *Tampa* becomes a starting point for a much wider journey of discovery. 'How can I, who am not a researcher of refugee issues, speak about the problem of the refugees beneath the bridge of the *Tampa*? The problem of the [Korean] Muslims, the problem of North Korea, and all sorts of issues appeared. They are all connected to the existence of "refugees"'.[31]

To bring these long-concealed presences 'on to the deck' — into the light of day — also requires a rethinking of time. One problem of the contemporary world, Lee suggests, is its emphasis on speed. Everything must be instantly labelled — as '11 September' or 'terrorism', for example; everything must be instantly responded to. Such speed makes impossible a proper recognition of refugees, whose lives operate in a different regime of time. 'The time of the refugee camp — the time of the refugee ship *Tampa* — greatly exceeds the time of the mainland. That is why, as this acceleration grows faster and faster, it becomes absolutely impossible to see refugees'.[32] The issue of 'recognising refugees', while it is a matter of legal recognition under international conventions, is thus also inescapably a deeper problem of 'recognising' the living presence of the refugee as a human being. 'In relation to the *Tampa* I likened the people [on the ship] to "cargo". The establishment of standards for recognising refugees is a problem of how we recognise that "cargo" as people'.[33]

Lee Chong-Hwa's reflections on the *Tampa* crisis cast a new light on the question of how 'they' (Japanese, Koreans, Chinese and so on) see 'us' (Australians). Indeed, her comments destabilise every aspect of that question. The notion of 'them' is no longer as simple as it seemed. 'Japanese images of Australia' are implicitly assumed to be perceptions expressed within the boundaries of the Japanese nation, usually in the Japanese language, by people who are Japanese by nationality and ethnicity. But increasingly, the images that circulate in the Japanese language, within and across the boundaries of Japan, include images created by those who, like Lee Chong-Hwa, are not Japanese by birth, ancestry or nationality. The 'seeing' is also generally assumed to be done from within Japan, through the window of Japanese media. But Lee, of course, 'sees' the *Tampa* from her room in London, mainly through the medium of the BBC and British newspapers.

But lastly and most importantly, the 'view of the world from the *Tampa*' deeply complicates the notion of 'us' as objects of scrutiny by 'them'. At one level, to be sure, I cannot read Lee's words without feeling deeply ashamed of the Australian Government's policies, and deeply sad that so few Australians were able to sense the seasickness and suffocation and suffering of the *Tampa* asylum-seekers. But at the same time the issue here is no longer simply whether 'they' approve or disapprove of 'us', whether 'their' criticisms of 'us' are correct, or whether 'they' are more or less humanitarian than 'us'.

The issue is how you and I can discover the threads of imagination and memory that create new forms of 'us', across as well as within national boundaries; how that re-imagining of 'us' can become (as it must be) also a process of unmaking the injustice and violence that reduce people to unwanted cargo — to flotsam and jetsam, discarded on the tide — to make our own journey though the storm more secure.

Lee's reflections, in other words, invite us not so much to consider how 'East Asians' see 'us' Australians, but how people in Australia and East Asia can begin to imagine and create together an 'us' capable of addressing problems of refugee recognition and human rights from which no one is unconnected. To do this requires an ability to wonder what has become of each of the 433 asylum-seekers rescued by the *Tampa*: where are they now? How do they remember the long days and nights on the ship, in the naval vessels, in the camps in Nauru and elsewhere? Are they haunted, as Lee is, by the memories of seasickness, heat, the struggle for air? What will become of them in the future?

Beyond that, her words invite you and me to attempt to create an 'us' which might also include the people on the *Tampa*, those who came after them, and those yet to come.

To quote the closing words of the *Sekai* interview: 'How do we make the people on the *Tampa* into people? How do we make into people those who are people and yet have not become people? We must put this into words, or else ... This, I think, is where the meaning of speech lies. We must give speech such meaning. I am a person, and you are a person too, and we are also people. In this, surely, lies the meaning of the law of nations and of international law'.[34]

Footnotes

1. Australia a World Leader in Managing Migration. Department of Immigration and Multiculturalism and Indigenous Affairs. Media release, 2002, MPS095/2002.
2. Woods, Denise. 2002. *Tampa* Tantrums: Charting the Media's response. Paper presented at the conference of the Asian Studies Association of Australia, Hobart, 1–3 July, 2002.
3. Isozaki, Yumi. 2002. Towareru 'Nanmin sakoku' Nihon. pp.143-50. *Sekai* 703. July, 2002. (An English translation entitled 'Questioning Japan's "Closed Country" Policy on Refugees' is available on *Sekai*'s English-language web site, *Japan in the World*, http://www.iwanami.co.jp/jpworld/text/ClosedCountry01.html)
4. The national newspapers included here are the daily broadsheets, but exclude the evening tabloids, which focus mainly on sports and entertainment. Except where otherwise indicated, all quotations are from the papers' morning editions.
5. *Asahi Shimbun*, 28 August, 2001.
6. *Mainichi Shimbun*, evening edition, 29 August, 2001.
7. *Sankei Shimbun*, 28 August, 2001.
8. *Nihon Keizai Shimbun*, 29 August, 2001.
9. *Sankei Shimbun*, 1 September, 2001; *Nihon Keizai Shimbun*, 1 September, 2001.
10. *Yomiuri Shimbun*, 1 September, 2001.
11. *Chunichi Shimbun*, 1 September, 2001; *Kobe Shimbun*, 1 September, 2001.
12. *Yomiuri Shimbun*, 5 September, 2001.
13. *Mainichi Shimbun*, 31 August, 2001.
14. *Mainichi Shimbun*, 2 September, 2001.
15. *Mainichi Shimbun*, 1 September, 2001.
16. *Asahi Shimbun*, 3 September, 2001.
17. *Asahi Shimbun*, 11 September, 2001.
18. *Asahi Shimbun*, 7 September, 2001.
19. *Asahi Shimbun*, evening edition, 17 January, 2002.
20. Ibid.
21. Isozaki, Towareru 'Nanmin sakoku' Nihon, p.146.
22. Lee, Chong-Hwa. 1998. *Tsubuyaki no seiji shiso*. Tokyo: Seidosha.
23. Lee, Chong-Hwa. 2002. Nanmin-sen *Tampa* kara mitsumeru sekai. pp.168–81. *Sekai* 703. July, 2002.
24. Ibid., pp.168–169.
25. Ibid., pp.169–170.
26. Ibid., p.169.

[27] Ibid., p.171.
[28] Ibid., p.170.
[29] Ibid., p.172.
[30] Ibid., p.177.
[31] Ibid., p.179.
[32] Ibid., p.174.
[33] Ibid., p.180.
[34] Ibid., p.181.

7. 'JAPANESE' ACCOUNTS OF AUSTRALIA

A PLAYER'S VIEW

Yoshio Sugimoto

It is awkward and uncomfortable to be the subject and the object of research at the same time. I have published two popular Japanese books on Australia, one of which (Sugimoto, 1991) went into 10 printings and is probably the best-selling book about Australian society on the Japanese market in the past few decades. I also contribute a regular column to the *Asahi Shimbun*, with a nation-wide circulation of eight million copies a day, and, for the past six years, have appeared fortnightly on a nation-wide radio program, *Rajio shinya-bin* (*Late Night Live*), on Japan's NHK Radio One, with a few million listeners. It is therefore difficult for me to be an objective investigator into how 'others' see Australia, because I am one of the players in the field — one of those 'others' — rather than a detached and disinterested umpire.

In the highly competitive Japanese publishing market, only a small segment of the market has any interest in reading about Australia: Americans — and to some extent Europeans — form the 'significant others' for most Japanese.[1] In this environment, it is not easy to produce publications on Australia which attract many readers. In the very broad field of non-academic, socio-cultural writings, two key dimensions stand out. First, the general objectives of writing — ranging from general entertainment purposes to more serious analyses of social structures. Second, is whether the target audience includes those who wish to travel to Australia or not. Combining these two variables, Figure 1 shows a four-fold diagram of socio-cultural writings about Australia for a Japanese readership (Figure 1).

Figure 1. Typology of Japanese socio-cultural writings about Australia

Type of Information Potential visit to Australia	for entertainment	for lifestyle and value change
No	(A) Accounts of exotic animals, sporting events	(D) Writings on civic practices
Yes	(B) Publications for tourism/hospitality	(C) Books and articles on education, working visa, migration and settlement

Cell A consists of the most popular representations of Australia which the entertainment industry disseminates chiefly via TV. Exotic animals, sporting events, the vast space and environment are cases in point. Cell B is also a huge sphere, as some 7,000 Japanese tourists visit here every year and they consume a large amount of entertainment images of Australia, which the hospitality industry propagates. Cell C concerns the domain of serious information for those who are interested in getting education, working and settling in Australia. Japanese migrants in Australia differ from other ethnic groups in coming here mainly for lifestyle reasons, not for economic or political reasons, with most intending to go back to Japan in the end.[2] In this context, books on Japanese expatriates, sojourners and long-term residents in Australia provide practical facts, data and advice about their life conditions and lifestyles here and have gained popularity as the number of Japanese desiring to settle overseas has increased.

My own work is primarily in Sphere D, addressing those who do not necessarily intend to visit but are interested in our civic practices. Many who read about the social systems and cultural practices of foreign countries are looking for clues that might lead to improvements in their own society — a society with which they are dissatisfied with some aspects. So, for example, Japanese read books about Australia's welfare system not to examine how deficient and awful it is, but to find inspirations about how to improve the Japanese counterpart. Japanese read books about Australian Aboriginal affairs not only to learn how depressing the Aborigine's situation is, but for a fresh perspective that might help to ameliorate the conditions of the indigenous Ainu population in Japan. Some Japanese writers produce case studies of schools and families in Australia as a mirror against which the Japanese readership can examine the Japanese situation.[3] When written with careful provisos and thoughtful qualifications, some of these books may reveal aspects of Australian civil society that can inform Japanese efforts at reforming their own civil society.

With this in mind, the topics on my radio program that received the greatest listener feedback can be classified into six categories as shown in Figure 2. For the past several months, debates in Australia have attracted some attention, including the Australian position on war with Iraq, Aboriginal history, asylum-seekers and their detention, and Arabs in Australia.

Figure 2. Some specific items which received much feedback from Japanese radio listeners

1. *Multiculturalism*

Point system for migration

Human Rights and Equal Opportunity Commission

Mabo ruling

Dual citizenship

2. *Gender issues*

Intervention orders to protect victims of family violence

In-school crèches for teenage mothers

Marriages between homosexuals

3. *Work and leisure*

Long-service leave

Do-it-yourself house renovation

4. *Civil society*

Prohibition of cigarette smoking in buildings and restaurants

Euthanasia

HECS system

5. *Legal framework*

Compulsory voting

Methods of name change

Absence of capital punishment

6. *Welfare and health issues*

Free public hospitals

Separation of dispensary from medical practice

Seeing-eye dogs

Every description of a foreign country contains implicit comparable propositions about the writer's home country. From the Japanese point of view, Ruth Benedict's renowned study, *The Chrysanthemum and the Sword* (1947), reads as her statement about American society by revealing the set of assumptions she makes about Japan.[4] Similarly, a number of books by Japanese authors about Australian multiculturalism assume — albeit implicitly — that Japanese society is not multicultural — or at least, not *as* multicultural — and can thus be read as statements about the authors' 'self-images'. The notion popular among Japanese business executives that Australia's industrial relations are conflict-ridden assumes a contrastive image — which they cherish — that Japan's labour relations are conflict-free. And when Japanese writers refer to the Australians' relaxed lifestyles, they reflect their own vision of the stressful and tense Japanese life. Regardless of whether these underlying images of Japan are correct or incorrect, the point here is that how 'others' see Australia reveals how they see their own society.

Since a majority of Japanese readers of books about Australian society are not looking for descriptions that preserve academically acceptable proportion, the challenge for a writer is to strike a balance in at least three areas. The first of these involves an understanding that good things come with bad, and vice versa: one must maintain a balance between the desirable and undesirable aspects of any given practice or convention. For example, what is perceived — with praise — to be the relaxed work attitude among Australian workers is closely connected to the often frustratingly inefficient standards of service and delivery. Some aspects of multiculturalism enable ethnic lobby groups to make claims about the homogeneity of fictitiously constructed ethnic cultures and can lead to ethnic groups forming their own ghettos. It might even be argued that the comfortable life conditions of some sections of the Australian community are to some extent derived from the exclusion and even exploitation and repression of certain types of refugees. Accounts of Australian society would be one-sided unless correlations between its bright and dark sides were taken into consideration.

The second challenge lies in the presentation of the particular and universal elements present in any society. Presumably unique Australian characteristics are rendered comprehensible through the use of functional alternatives and universalist terminology, thus avoiding the pitfalls of occidentalism and exoticism. Japanese readers can understand the significance of Vegemite in Australia when they think of their own *nattō*. The practice of sending Christmas cards in Australia is functionally equivalent to that of mailing New Year's cards in Japan. Ned Kelly's story makes sense to the many Japanese readers familiar with the story of Nezumi Kozō Jirōkichi, a folk figure in feudal Japan, who reportedly stole money from the mansions of feudal lords in Tokyo and distributed it to poor people. Australian legends of half-man and half-animal yowies remind some Japanese of *yukionna* legends, popular narratives of snow fairies in various parts of Japan. Communications across national boundaries are often facilitated by apparent commonalities and resemblances shared by people with different backgrounds, rather than through an emphasis on cultural differences and divergences.

Thirdly, authors describing the social and cultural characteristics of a given society must be clear about the representativeness of their samples, and the extent to which it is fair to generalise the patterns apparent in a given sample to the society at large. National stereotyping is the enemy of comparative analysis. For example, it would be wrong to define Australia as a health-conscious society on the basis of observations restricted to the educated urban middle class. It would be equally incorrect to categorise Australia generally as a racist society only on the basis of the current Aboriginal situation.

This sampling question compels us to explicitly address the question of who we define as 'Australian'. The theme of this conference, 'as others see us', is problematic to the extent that the conceptual boundary of 'Australian' remains undefined. Since the criteria for defining 'Australian' would involve many dimensions — such as citizenship, residency, socialisation, language and self-identification — it is not always easy to include or exclude individuals such as Rupert Murdoch, who was born and raised in Australia but lives overseas and does not hold an Australian passport; an Italian migrant who has Australian citizenship but cannot speak English; or a teenage child of Australian parents who has lived in Japan since birth and does not see himself as Australian. The definition of Australian contracts or expands depending on whether it is based upon an exclusivist or inclusivist framework. I relish a kind of dual existence as a naturalised Australian citizen who is identified by others more often than not as ethnically Japanese. An inclusive approach, which I favour, compels me to think of 'how others see us' in terms of 'how I see myself'.

Finally, I would like to caution against an over-emphasis on textual analysis — the dominant methodology in contemporary studies of how 'others' see Australia. Writing is undoubtedly an exercise in image formation, category creation and theory construction, for which textual analysis remains indispensable. Publishing, however, is not simply editorial production; it includes commercial distribution and voluntary consumption, important variables that have received little attention compared with the intensity with which the contents and substance of each text are analysed. Little is known about which sectors of Japanese society consume which types of images of, and books about, Australia or of how these images are received. I therefore suggest that an examination of the sociological attributes of the widely varied Japanese readership of a range of books about Australian society would more fruitfully shed light on how 'others' see Australia — in particular, who 'cherishes' certain visions of Australia and why. Who are the enthusiastic consumers of images of Australian native animals? Which groups avidly read books about Australian multiculturalism? Which social strata tend to be interested in Australia's welfare systems?

Critical studies of *Nihonjinron* (writings about the 'essential qualities' of the Japanese) have established some precedents on similar issues. For example, a comparative analysis of readers of this genre of books has revealed that businessmen use them as tools to justify their international negotiating techniques, while school teachers study them to redress the 'negative Japanese qualities'.[5] Other research has demonstrated that housewives generally have more universalistic and less nationalistic views about their own society than male company employees.[6]

These studies of consumer behaviour reveal that 'others' are not a uniform or homogeneous entity, but are varied in their social background and their interpretations of texts. So long as it is agreed that 'we' and 'they' are diverse and stratified, studies of how 'others see us' that do not consider the various material conditions of readers and their consumption patterns will remain deficient.

Footnotes

1. In the 1980s, Keisō Shobō made a conscious effort to publish books on Australia and launched a series on Australia. The project proved a commercial disaster despite support from the Australia-Japan Foundation. Keisō ceased to publish the series after bringing several titles into print.
2. Satō, Machiko. 2002. *Farewell to Nippon: Japanese Lifestyle Migrants in Australia*. Melbourne: Trans Pacific Press.
3. Satō, Machiko. 1987. *Onna-tachi no Ōsutoraria (Women's Australia)*. Tokyo: Keisō Shobō. Satō, Machiko. 1994. *Gorei no nai gakkō: Ōsutoraria no kyōiku kankaku (Schools Without Military Attention: Education Styles in Australia)*. Tokyo: Chikuma Shobō. Satō, Machiko. 1996. *Koara no kuni de kurashite mitara (Living in a Koala Country)*. Tokyo: Chikuma Shobō. Satō, Machiko. 1999. *Bai ringaru Japaniizu (Bilingual Japanese)*. Kyoto: Jinbun Shoin.
4. Kuwayama, Takami. 2003. Reverse Ethnography. Chapter 5. *Native Anthropology: Japanese Challenge to Western Academic Hegemony*. Melbourne: Trans Pacific Press.
5. Yoshino, Kosaku. 1992. *Cultural Nationalism in Contemporary Japan*. London: Routledge.
6. Mabuchi, Hitoshi. 2002. *'Ibunka rikai' no disukōsu: bunka honshitsu shugi no otoshiana (Discourse on 'Foreign Culture Understanding': Pitfalls of Cultural Essentialism)*. Kyoto: Kyoto University Press.

Further references

Sugimoto, Yoshio. 1991. *Ōsutoraria rokusen-nichi (Six Thousand Days of Living in Australia)*. Tokyo: Iwanami Shoten.

Sugimoto, Yoshio. 2000. *Ōsutoraria: Tabunka shakai no sentaku (Australia: Its Choice of Multiculturalism)*. Tokyo: Iwanami Shoten.

8. READING JAPANESE REFLECTIONS OF AUSTRALIA

Masayo Tada

What interests me in reading Japanese accounts of Australia is the comparative perspectives that generate them. When Japanese authors express their impressions of Australia, these impressions are inevitably based on their comparisons of Australia and Japan. In other words, these authors' reflections of Australia, in fact, also reflect what they identified as Japaneseness.

Considering comparative perspectives in these accounts, I would like to suggest that Japanese accounts of Australia can be important sources for an understanding of Japanese and Australian societies and for the examination of various transnational issues. I will elaborate on this by introducing some Japanese authors' reflections of gender issues in Australia.

Firstly, these accounts can be interesting material to study about Japan. To my mind, it is far more important to consider why Japanese people hold or express certain impressions of Australia, than trying to judge the accuracy of their portrait of Australia. Japanese reflections of Australia can be investigated through an examination of a writer's gender, age, socio-economic status and historical circumstances associated with the production of the material. Such investigation will also involve the examination of Japanese assumptions about Japaneseness. Thus Japanese accounts of Australia can be a point of departure for further studies of Japanese society.

Let me give you some examples of Japanese reflections of gender issues in Australia since the 1970s. The authors of writings on Australian society published in the 1970s were mainly government officials, business people and journalists who had opportunities to work in Australia for a period of time. They tended to be the well-educated male élite of Japanese society, and some of them represented Australian husbands as family men who contributed much to housework. Oikawa Kineo was a 35-year-old exchange NHK (*Nihon Hōsō Kyōkai*: Japan Broadcasting Corporation) broadcaster with the ABC in Melbourne between 1971 and 1973.[1] In his accounts of social life and people in Melbourne, he represents Australian husbands as being domesticated and dominated by their wives, and expresses surprise and sympathy for them.[2] This is common in some Japanese male writings on Australia in the 1970s, and remains potent in Japanese images of the 'Australian husband' to the extent that the term has these specific connotations.[3]

Gender relations in Australia were thus represented as otherness to what they identified as Japanese gender relations, and this representation was also evident in the next decades. Beginning in the 1980s more female authors produced accounts of Australia. These authors were often those with children who came to Australia due to their husband's work, and their writings focus on issues such as education and women's status in Australia in comparison with Japan.[4] Because of an increasing number of male expatriate employees of Japanese institutions living overseas with their wives and children, the issues concerning overseas life and returnee children became more salient social issues in Japan.[5] Ogata Masako lived in Sydney for five years with her three-year-old daughter, accompanying her husband who worked there, and wrote about her life in Sydney with a focus on raising her child. Ogata remarks on education free of pressure and husbands and wives relating as equal partners in her book published in 1982. Satō Machiko, who has lived in Australia since 1973 with her husband and children, produced three books on Australia in the 1980s.[6] She depicts education and the social conditions of women in Australia favourably in comparison with Japan. Satō discusses an education in Australia that focuses on cultivating students' individuality and creativity, the relatively equal gender relations, and independent youth, and criticises Japanese education that focuses on rote-learning and controlling students, women's subservient status, and youths' dependence on their parents.[7]

In the 1990s, with an increase in the number of Japanese visiting or living in Australia, authors of accounts of Australia were more diverse, including travellers, housewives, exchange students, Japanese language teachers and migrants. Many such essays focus not only on their cross-cultural experience, but their search for self. It was popular for Japanese women to study and travel abroad to the extent that Japanese women who lived in foreign countries outnumbered Japanese men in 1999.[8] Female accounts of the social conditions of women in Australia continued to be produced through the 1990s, and they tended to represent Australia as a care-free country.[9] These authors lived and travelled in the country for a relatively long period when they were in their twenties. Mothers who travelled and lived in Australia with their children represented Australia as a place where they could rediscover their own self without the social pressure and restrictions they felt in Japan.[10] Okumura Noriko, a single mother who travelled and lived in Australia with her daughter, represented Australia as a place where she could be herself because in Australia there were very few social restrictions on women and mothers. She feels that a single mother tends to be treated as an aberration in Japan.[11]

To understand continuing interests in gender issues in Australia expressed in Japanese accounts of Australia between the 1970s and the 1990s, it is useful to look at some statistical data. In Japan, a survey on time use and leisure has been conducted every five years since 1976. In 1976, 30- to 39-year-old husbands with children spent nine minutes on housework and childcare and five minutes shopping per day. A similar survey has been carried out in Australia every five years since 1992. Making a comparison of Japan and Australia, time spent per day on housework and related work (childcare, nursing and shopping) was, in Japan, 24 minutes by men and 332 minutes by women in 1991, and, in Australia, 150 minutes by men and 291 minutes by women in 1992.[12] Although we should consider a variety of other issues in investigating Japanese reflections of gender issues in Australia, including Japanese assumptions about Japan, the continuing gender gap in time spent on housework in Japan provides part of the explanation of the ways in which some Japanese authors wrote about gender issues in Australia.

In looking at these comparative data, while some Australian women may not agree, for instance, with Japanese representations of the Australian husband, it is quite understandable that some Japanese people viewed the Australian husband as being a great contributor to housework. It would also be interesting to compare situations of single mothers in Australia and Japan to understand why some Japanese single mothers somehow felt more comfortable in Australia.

This leads to my second point, that Japanese accounts of Australia can also be important sources for understanding Australia through cross-cultural comparative analyses. Although I talked only about gender issues here, these accounts are rich sources of other interesting topics for cross-cultural comparison.

This relates to my third point. These topics can also be seen as transnational topics, which aren't topics relevant only to Australia and Japan. By looking at societies comparatively, we are able to deepen our understanding. However, I strongly feel that there is a need to overcome the kinds of comparisons based on stereotypical assumptions about certain countries or regions, such as the conventional opposition between the West and the East. A kind of comparative perspective that makes us reconsider our own assumptions about national or regional characteristics is very important. For example, Japanese portraits of Australia provide a chance for reflecting on assumptions about Australia and Japan, and seeing the two countries with fresh eyes.

To conclude, Japanese accounts of Australia selected for English translation in this project can be useful for encouraging people to study further about many interesting transnational issues in the contexts of Australia and Japan. If these accounts were read simply as generalised Japanese-typical images of Australia, this would be rather a retreat from a better understanding of Australian and Japanese societies as part of an increasingly transnational world.

Footnotes

[1] Japanese names are given in the East Asian order — family name followed by given or personal name.

[2] Oikawa Kineo. 1975. *Meruborun nōto*. Tokyo: Nihon Hōsō Shuppankai.

[3] For example, in a book on Australia published in 1990, two contributors refer to the Japanese myth of the 'Australian husband'. Nakano Fujio (ed.). 1990. *Motto shiritai Osutoraria*. pp.117, 135. Tokyo: Kōbundō.

[4] Amaya Kimiko. 1986. *Tondetta būmeran: Amaya-ke no kaigai kikoku shijo kyōiku funsenki*. Tokyo: Kumon Shuppan. Endō Masako. 1983. *Shidonî no gogo: My Days in Australia*. Tokyo: Sanshūsha. Nakajima Yōko. 1984. *Sunde mita Osutoraria: rika kyōshi no kansatsu nōto*. Tokyo: Saimaru Shuppankai. Ogata Masako. 1982. *Shidonî no nonbiri kosodate: Osutoraria no aozora no shita de*. Tokyo: Chūō Kōronsha. Haruko Robinson. 1983. *Mai Osutoraria: zaigō 18-nen no jānarisuto ga kataru sugao no rakkī kantorī*. Tokyo: Jakku Bokkusu.

[5] The number of Japanese nationals living abroad for more than three months and permanent expatriates, including those with dual nationality, had increased from 445,372 in 1980 to 620,174 in 1990. Japanese Statistics Bureau. 2001. *Japan Statistical Yearbook*. p.54. As for the number of Japanese children at the compulsory education age living abroad, it had dramatically increased from 27,465 in 1980 to 49,336 in 1990. Japanese Ministry of Education, Culture, Sports, Science and Technology. Education for Japanese Children living overseas and returnee children. 27 September, 2001 (cited 3 February, 2003), available at http://www.mext.go.jp/english/org/exchange/10e.htm

[6] Satō Machiko. 1985. *Ōsutoraria kara no tegami: sunde wakatta koseiha kyoiku to nobinobi kurashi*. Tokyo: Gakuyō Shoin. Satō Machiko. 1987. *Onnatachi no Ōsutoraria*. Tokyo: Keisō Shobō. Satō Machiko. 1989. *Gōorei no nai gakkō: Ōsutoraria no kyôiku kankaku*. Tokyo: Gakuyō Shobō.

[7] Satō Machiko. 1985. *Ōsutoraria kara no tegami*. It should be noted that in the 1980s Japanese people increasingly discussed in the educational reform debates the need to shift school education from cramming and competition to creativity and a more relaxed approach.

[8] The *Asahi Shimbun* reported that Japanese women who lived in foreign countries had outnumbered Japanese men in 1999 for the first time since the commencement of the survey in 1976 (402,575

women and 393,277 men). Kaigai ni sumu nihonjin josei, dansei nuku: ryūgaku, NGO katsudō ikigai sagashi. p.2. *Asahi Shimbun*, 8 May, 2000. It is observed in the article that the major factor of the reversal was an increase in the number of women who pursued a meaningful life overseas by engaging in study or volunteer and NGO activities. The rate of increase of the number of Japanese women going to the Oceania region was 15.3 per cent compared with that in the previous year, which was the largest increase rate.

9 In an ethnographic account of Japanese settlers in Australia, Satō Machiko describes recent Japanese settlers in Australia as 'lifestyle migrants' (*seishin imin*, literally 'spiritual migrants'), who desire to improve their quality of life in various ways, including by having a more easygoing, carefree life abroad. Satō Machiko. 1993. *Shin kaigai teijū jidai: Ōsutoraria no Nihonjin*. Tokyo: Shinchōsha. The English version of this book is *Farewell to Nippon: Japanese Lifestyle Migrants in Australia*, 2001, Melbourne: Trans Pacific Press.

10 Kitazawa Aiko. 1990. *Harukanaru ao tea roa: Nyūjīrando, Ōsutoraria boshi taizaiki*. Osaka: Shinbun Insatsu Shuppan Sentâ. Naruse Mayumi. 1997. *Itsudatte jibun sagashi: Ōsutoraria kozure ryūgaku ki*. Tokyo: WAVE Shuppan.

11 Okumura Noriko. 1993. *Fūten mama no Ōsutoraria*. Tokyo: Gakuyō Shobō. Saitō Kiyoko. 1992. *Shidonî karāchi shîn (Sydney's Cultural Scene)*. Sydney: Shakai Shisōsha.

12 Japanese Statistics Bureau. 1978. *Japan Statistical Yearbook*. pp.598–99. 1993–94. *Japan Statistical Yearbook*. pp.728–29. Australian Bureau of Statistics. 1992. *How Australians Use Their Time*. p.8.

9. ASIAN AUSTRALIAN STUDIES IN ASIA: CHINA AND JAPAN

David Carter

This essay rests on two assumptions. First, that 'cultural diplomacy' is a good thing. Second, that 'Australian studies' have a significant role to play in cultural diplomacy. Both points, of course, need elaboration and qualification. In providing this I want to talk about the situation of Australian studies in China and Japan, their strengths but also weaknesses in having any significant influence on 'how others see us'.

By cultural diplomacy, I mean the process of deliberately — that is, as a matter of policy and supported by government money and infrastructure — 're-purposing' Australian cultural products, whether books, art, dance, theatre, craft, music or their creators, as a means of telling the rest of the world something about Australia, past, present and future. Cultural diplomacy by definition means working within a government agenda, and for that reason the idea often produces a negative response from those in the academy, especially those at the 'cultural' end of the academy. This reaction, I believe, is often little more than a residual form of late-romantic 'culturalism' — the belief that culture transcends the more sordid domains of market-place or policy-making.

My argument is that we must take on board the positive case for engagement with cultural diplomacy and that those

I might call 'cultural academics' or 'cultural intellectuals' have an important role to play in shaping how the nation thinks about and projects itself and in shaping the reception of these projections outside Australia. Having said that, one of the key intellectual and cultural benefits of engaging in this process is that the reception never can be determined or shaped definitively; the process will always involve conflicting perceptions and frameworks and we should expect to be rudely reminded at times just how Australia looks from elsewhere.

Although we will always want to reserve the right to be sceptical of any (and every) government's immediate motives — the resistance and debate is part of the process — the agenda and procedures of cultural diplomacy are normally broad enough to enable all sorts of engagements to occur within their brief. And they are mostly operated by 'arm's-length' bodies. Most of us, I would guess, could find ways of taking on board the desire of government to project Australia abroad as a sophisticated, multicultural, democratic nation (according to the present rhetoric). After all, talking publicly about racism and intolerance would be one mark of such a society — at least in my reading.

In other words, we need to talk to government, to work with government, to lobby government, not to walk away and accuse government for, well, being government.

What about the role of Australian studies? Side-stepping for the moment the question of just what Australian studies are, promoting the study of Australia at all levels of the curriculum and supporting serious research on Australia overseas seems to have a crucial role not just in producing 'foreign friends' who think better of us, but more importantly, in furthering the process of 'Asianising Australia'. I share Stephen FitzGerald's line on this, that 'Asianising Australia' in one sense just means '*Australianising* Australia' — coming to a fuller understanding of Australia's own history and its place in the world.[1] By the same token, by 'Asianising Australia' I mean the process of enmeshing Australia into regional and comparative perspectives, so that it becomes part of the picture, always within the frame, when models are sought, comparisons made and so forth. In fact, in this sense I wouldn't mind all that much being accused of wanting to 'Australianise *Asia*'.

Although I will argue against promoting Australian studies simply under the rubric of area studies (though I will if I have to), I do think there are advantages in promoting something explicitly called 'Australian studies' rather than just relying on the diffusion of Australian content or methodologies across the curriculum. This has strategic advantages — not least for teachers and researchers overseas within their own institutions — and is significant in the process of working with government. The key is not to define Australian studies narrowly or to erect high walls around the area but instead, as I will explain later, to see it as a vehicle for interdisciplinarity, methodological innovation, comparative studies and internationalisation. Later I'll be raising the issue of the lack of serious *research* on Australia from overseas; while this might be happening in specific areas such as foreign policy, economics or the environment, those much more slippery areas such as culture, society, politics and history, those that provide a deep, contextualised understanding, need the kind of framing that something like Australian studies can provide.

I also don't mind being accused of ignoring Europe and North America. In a sense, while it is nice to see Australian studies centres sprouting up from London to Moscow, I don't think Australian studies matter in quite the same way outside Asia or the Asia–Pacific region (and by that I mean 'matters to us' here in Australia and 'matters to them' in the region). This is partly because a more or less shared tradition of academic practice and research protocols means that Australian studies in Europe and North America can, as it were, look after themselves (in an intellectual sense if not in terms of funding or infrastructure support); and also partly because the consequences for Australia are less significant. To put it another way: who cares what the English think of Australia? I do care what the Chinese and Japanese think (and what the Americans think — but that's another argument).

I'm not going to attempt to describe what Chinese and Japanese Australianists think of Australia — that's a fascinating topic in its own right and one which others have researched (see Masayo Tada's paper). Instead I want to talk more about the programs of support from the Australian side for Australian studies in China and Japan — what's been done well, where the shortcomings lie and what might be done in the future. I will also make some remarks about how we might conceive of Australian studies in order for it to work most effectively in the region.

The readiest comparison to hand for Australian studies abroad is Canada and the Canadian Government's support of Canadian studies overseas. Last time I researched, a few years back, it appeared that the Canadian Government was spending about seven million Canadian dollars annually on programs supporting Canadian studies overseas, largely through their equivalent of our Department of Foreign Affairs and Trade (DFAT). This was seen to be a central part of the external affairs portfolio — with, it is true, some of the disadvantages as well as the many advantages of being centralised and bureaucratically integrated. As many will be aware, the Canadian Government supports an extensive program of grants and fellowships for overseas students and academics wishing to undertake Canadian studies and to teach and research Canada from elsewhere. Those of us working in Australian studies overseas are all too familiar with the question, why doesn't the Australian Government have a scheme like the Canadian Government?

Some quick calculations suggest that the Australian Federal Government spends a long way short of $1 million on Australian studies overseas, and that's including estimates for permanent staff salaries. There is one important exception to this statement which I'll come back to later. Whatever the exact amount is, more than half of it would be directed towards China and Japan — a correct bias, I think, even if the amounts are relatively small. Of course, if we add in other agencies involved in cultural diplomacy — the Australia Council, the

Australian International Cultural Council and Asialink, for example — the budget grows. But the dedicated Australian studies budget remains small.

We must be thankful for DFAT or rather for the bilateral bodies that manage the Australian studies programs: the Australia–China Council, the Australia–Japan Foundation and their counterparts for India, Indonesia and Korea.

At this point in time, the federal department responsible for education — DEST — does nothing at all, a fact we notice because in the mid-1990s, for a short time before and a very short time after the election of the present Federal Government, the Department of Education (DEETYA as it was then called) had a dedicated program and a federal committee of bureaucrats and academics established to oversee a program for Australian studies offshore — and its focus was almost entirely on Asia.[2]

The outcome of that program, under former Ministers Vanstone and Kemp, was a series of valuable country reports that have never been made public, a few one-off, short-term projects, all long gone, and two $5 million allocations to two overseas Australian studies centres: yes, you guessed it, one in London and one in Washington. These weren't straight-out gifts — as I understand it, the centres get to live off the interest of the endowments. Still, the priorities were revealing. (This is the important exception I mentioned earlier.)

Let me summarise briefly the kinds of support provided for Australian studies in China and Japan. These are the two most mature of the Australian studies networks overseas. There are two ways to tell the story of Australian studies in China and Japan — a 'good news' story and a 'bad news' story. Both are valid but depend upon the framework or perspective we adopt. The former shows a high level of achievement built on small resources and commitment from the Australian side. The latter tells a story of minimal 'high level' achievement, especially in the area of top-quality research about Australia. I'll begin with the good news.

China

The Australia–China Council (ACC) supports 15 Australian studies centres at last count, from Guangzhou to Inner Mongolia. These vary greatly — some are not much more than a single academic staff member, a title on the door and a 'trophy' shelf of book gifts from the Australian Government or visiting academics. Others have Masters-level teaching programs and staff engaged in research; the Academies of Social Science in Beijing and Shanghai are full research institutions although Australia competes for attention with many other nations.

There are other programs as well operated by the ACC: support for buying resources, book and translation awards; support for the Chinese Australian Studies Association and its biennial conference; and, most significant perhaps, a scheme of fellowships and scholarships enabling Chinese academic and graduate students to spend time in Australia, usually for six weeks to a few months. These are competitive, based on academic merit and the strength of a research proposal.

Trends in the ACC support for these programs are perhaps indicative of trends in government more generally. Increasingly, funding support is performance- and/or project-based rather than recurrent funding — i.e. the centres must now make a claim to competitive project funding rather than expect to receive regular funding as a matter of course. The management of the whole 'Australian Studies in China' program has recently been put out to tender — in effect, for outsourcing — and here I must declare a conflict of interest, as the Australian studies centre which I direct has recently been announced as the successful tender.

If this sounds like economic rationalism there are good reasons behind these shifts, too: the shift to competitive project funding is designed to focus on performance and track record in general but also, more specifically, to give a much greater emphasis to *research* output. Along with the Japanese perhaps, Chinese Australian studies are probably the only network mature enough to benefit from this kind of shift at present.

The majority of the Chinese Australian studies centres began in English or foreign-language departments which meant some bias until recently towards literary studies or 'cultural' and historical studies with something of an over-reliance on literary texts. This has shifted in recent times with more research being done into indigenous issues, multiculturalism, environmental issues, media, politics and so forth. I thought it a positive sign at the most recent Chinese Australian Studies Association conference, at Anhui University in Hefei in 2002, that I could hear a paper on Australian sewerage systems as well as papers on David Malouf, media ownership or mateship.

Given this past, Australian studies in China have been largely an English-language affair. The majority of papers at conferences have been delivered in English — a great boon to those of us struggling with beginner's Mandarin — and most courses are taught within English departments and often in English. Graduate students tend to be citizens of the English-language electronic world and, increasingly, are tuned in to global research agendas. While the dominance of English has, at least in theory, meant more direct access by Chinese students and researchers to English-language sources, and more access for Australians to Chinese Australian studies materials in English, it has also reinforced some limits on the building of Australian studies as an interdisciplinary enterprise and limited its potential influence across the universities and research centres. One of the biggest difficulties facing researchers in China is not just finding the resources for research, not just getting it published, but getting any reasonable kind of distribution or circulation of published research. Australian studies remain rather isolated, in an enclave, often relying on the heroic efforts of an individual or two in an institution, rather than being part of an academic or intellectual mainstream (although, as I will have to repeat later, there are exceptions). One of the present imperatives of the ACC is to increase the quantity of Chinese-language research and teaching about Australia.

Japan

The Australia–Japan Foundation (AJF) is the best-funded of the bilateral bodies. It has the luxury of a permanent officer in Tokyo and its budget helps to maintain an Australian Resource Centre in the Tokyo embassy which is probably one of the best general-use libraries for Australian studies outside Australia. It is used heavily by academics, students, members of the public and expat Aussies to catch up on the cricket score. It is now also heavily involved in remote, electronic requests for information, resource lending, etc. The AJF is part-funded by an endowment which means it does not have to rely solely on annual budget allocations from the Federal Government. It has its own Act of Parliament through which the foundation was established. The other important part of the program is a Chair in Australian Studies recently relocated in the Centre for American and Pacific Studies at Tokyo University (if this location sounds odd it is, in fact, a great benefit — Australian studies are not located within the English department or associated with language teaching! They are located within a research unit with a comparative and regional focus). This is a one-year rotating position.

After helping establish an Australian studies network in Japan a number of years ago, the program was languishing (and the Australian studies network was ageing) until a couple of years back when the AJF board put in place a new range of programs similar in many respects to the Chinese program, including book and translation awards and a scheme of fellowships and scholarships.

More recently, the AJF has moved to establish a serious electronic presence for Australian studies on its sophisticated web site, launching an Australian studies e-bulletin to inform Japanese Australianists of conferences, publications, grants and so forth.

There are two or three centres for Australian studies in Japan, but, unlike China, they are not a main focus for the foundation's programs. They have been focused largely on economic and trade issues, although the newest, at Waseda, has a more cultural focus. There is also a Japanese Australian Studies Association.

One of the key differences between China and Japan is that in Japan Australian studies have (again, until recently) had a strong bias towards trade and economic issues. They have not been predominantly grounded in English or foreign-language departments and, therefore, the second major difference from China, they have been largely in the Japanese language. This has had its own limiting effects as there has been limited communication between Japanese and Australian Australianists and virtually none between Japan and other parts of global Australian studies!

Australian studies are, in fact, taught widely across the Japanese system, in one form or another: 83 universities, more than 170 courses, taught to about 15,000 students. But these figures exaggerate the effect as the courses are usually at a fairly junior level, usually as part of something else, often as a quick introduction for students about to go to Australia for study tours. The teaching is usually not something driven by research interests, not in the prestigious parts of the academy, often not part of a degree structure.

I've been focusing on the universities, but in fact the foundation's biggest successes have been in secondary and primary education where it has produced Australian studies kits. The secondary school kit has been placed in more than 11,000 Japanese schools and follow-up programs with teachers have ensured its widespread use. This breakthrough into the relatively closed Japanese education system is a major achievement.

Australian studies trends

This is the good news story. Australia can point to a remarkable achievement in the form of Australian studies centres and conferences, translations, courses and graduate students, all on the basis of modest financial support. In this sense we might say that Australia is punching above its weight (though not if we consider the importance of these countries to Australia's future).

The not-so-good news story is that despite all this activity, some of it going back more than a decade, the number of serious courses taught is still very small, the number of students proceeding through to graduate studies on Australian topics is miniscule, and, perhaps most serious of all, the amount of serious, substantial, international-quality research is, with only a few exceptions, negligible.

In other words, there has been a failure to produce a substantial body of up-to-date top-quality research from among Asian Australianists. I am very conscious of some exceptions, for example, some excellent papers from younger researchers at the last Chinese Australian studies conference — so we might be able to predict a positive trend — but still, if we were summing up the picture so far, we'd have to say that very little research has been produced. Much of what has been produced has been at a very rudimentary level; and, despite the centres, the associations and the conferences, there is only a small number of active programs of research. And the research that is produced tends to have limited circulation, a limited influence, so that it is difficult to talk about a developing 'field' of Australian studies in these countries. There have been many books written in Japan about Australia, for example, but only a small number from a scholarly research perspective. And again, the problem of distribution has been significant.

Of course, there are clear reasons for this situation:

- There has until recently been little of what those in, say, Australian or American universities know as a 'research culture' in the humanities/social science areas;
- There has until recently been little research funding in the humanities/social science areas;
- The absence of a research culture is especially the case where Australian studies have emerged out of English-language teaching departments — which have been primarily devoted to language teaching;
- The problem of resources, of course, is perennial — there are few resources, few up-to-date sources of information, little access to current debates within *Australian* Australian studies, though this gap is decreasing with the use of electronic resources;

- More serious is the lack of an audience for serious research, lack of opportunities for publication of serious research, and lack of distribution and promotion of books that have been published. Research languishes — it often doesn't seem even to reach other Australianists;
- The lack of institutional support for Australian studies (one reason why government support from the Australian end is crucial);
- Ageing Australian studies networks — older academics from a less research-oriented era — and difficulties, in an increasingly competitive education environment, attracting younger graduate students and academics towards Australian studies;
- Hierarchical staffing structures which make it difficult for young staff to move into new areas;
- America — that's where all the students want to go, even those who've done an Australian studies MA tend to want to use it to get an American PhD;
- And, by the same token, Australia's 'minority' position — it is not a 'prestigious' culture in the academy as well as beyond in relation to the US or the main European nations; it is not seen as the originator of culture (one of the reasons we need Australian studies).

Where there is good research being done at graduate level it generally hasn't translated into new energies — new, younger academic staff — moving into the broader field of Australian studies and staying there. Perhaps this doesn't matter; I'm ambivalent myself. Perhaps exposure to Australian materials and methodologies at undergraduate and graduate level will, in most cases, be the most that can realistically be expected and achieves important aims in any case. But some of the best and brightest of the next generation of researchers do need to be 'Australianised' somewhere along the line.

One of the difficulties is that I don't think we will get any very serious attention from Australian governments — in lobbying for support for Australian studies overseas — until we are able to show that serious research *is* being produced. We are in danger of being caught in a catch-22: no serious funding until there is serious research, no serious research until there is serious funding. Frankly, there's little credibility at the moment, little that we could take to government and say 'look what's been achieved; give us a million dollars to do more of it'. I don't think an article or two on Judith Wright or *Crocodile Dundee* are going to help much here — though with the present government we might get a bit further with Les Murray.

Of course, Australian studies will keep finding a home in the English-language and literature departments, and so they should. Literature, cinema and other cultural forms will remain central to the enterprise. What we need to do is to push the boundaries of Australian studies out further, shift into new areas; but even more importantly try to think of new structures, new relationships, new funding mechanisms such that the emphasis shifts towards research, the research is up-to-date, and it is distributed, made accessible, built into teaching and research programs.

Of course, I have a wish list. I would like to see an expanded DEST-run scheme of graduate scholarships specifically designated for studies of Australia — not just study in Australia. A small number, as low as five a year from the Asia–Pacific region, could make a real difference. A Colombo Plan for the 21st century, perhaps, with an explicit Australian studies twist. I would also like to see more funding directed to commissioned research, probably through competitive bidding, including, but not limited to, areas where the Australian side can set the research priorities. But the point remains research by those offshore (in collaboration, of course, where appropriate) for their local and, wherever possible, for international audiences. I'd like to see a dedicated transnational program not only for bringing Asian Australianists to Australia but bringing people from different countries together. I would like to see some serious, coordinated investment in web-based and other resources for overseas scholars studying Australia — the online Japanese-language Australian studies bulletin is an important model.

Ideas of Australia

Despite the positive signs of new activity within the DFAT bilateral bodies,[3] and the pockets of Australian studies activity across the Asian region, the big picture is a pretty disheartening one. Research, in particular, has been at a minimal level. There is precious little evidence of Australian studies research that could, for example, impact on the way overseas governments and bureaucracies think about Australia. In fact, if we think of the level of Australian studies knowledge in most places in the region, it is positively scary to imagine the quality of information that overseas governments are getting about anything other than trade figures. The stereotypes of 'East versus West' are alive and well, even within Australian studies circles.

In this respect, on the basis of my own overseas experience teaching Australian studies and developing Australian studies centres, I argue strongly that Australian studies overseas should not be thought of — or sold as — yet another case of 'area studies'. This is mostly how Australian studies are perceived when they are parachuted into foreign universities. I'd want to make the case, instead, for seeing Australia, not as a vehicle for specialisation but for internationalisation. In other words, Australian studies promoted and pursued as part of regional studies, comparative studies, international studies, global studies — the emphasis will be different depending on the local context. Of course, we still want experts, specialists, researchers, centres, but how the project is conceived from the ground up makes a difference to how we might also conceive of these experts and specialists.

For many people working in overseas universities this is a matter of beginning from where they are — from existing research or teaching interests in American, British or Canadian societies, international law, foreign policy, social policy, women's studies and so forth — rather than attempting the leap into a whole new speciality. The important objective is not so much to produce full-time Australianists as to get Australia 'into the frame', to get it into the conversation, to incorporate it into comparative, regional, international frameworks — and, in many ways, that means emphasising what it shares with other nations rather than flogging its 'uniqueness'.

The way to conceive of the offshore development of Australian studies is not to focus on Australia in isolation or to imagine that we are beginning from nothing, but rather to think of Australia as belonging in a network of potential points of comparison and contrast — with the US and Europe in some dimensions, other colonial settler colonies in another, other Asia–Pacific nations in another and so on. The aim is to have Australia take its place naturally in the frameworks of comparison in whatever the field is — literature, geography, anthropology, public health, environmental policy and so on.

From this perspective we have to be prepared to allow for the possibility that the best 'Australian studies' won't always come from within the field explicitly named as such — this is certainly the case in Australia itself. Allowing this also allows us the possibility of seeing Australian studies as linked to the idea of Australia as a place ideas come from — not just products or tourists. Australia is a significant exporter of research, theories, knowledge and culture (to return to my opening theme), an originator, in areas as diverse as women's studies, cultural studies, environmental studies, international law, indigenous studies and, of course, Asian studies. Australian studies need to be open enough to let in all of these developments.

From another perspective, Australian studies are a massively under-utilised resource — under-utilised, that is, by Australian governments, and perhaps even by our own universities supposedly committed to the internationalisation of education and promoting a positive image of the nation. 'Studying in Australia' is almost completely disarticulated from 'studying Australia' — certainly there is no structured program to encourage that further step.

The Asian Accounts of Australia Project itself poses some interesting questions about how the research it has generated could feed back into Australian studies in China and Japan and elsewhere in the region. At first I thought 'minimally'; after all, isn't our primary task that of increasing the overseas study of Australian materials? But on reflection, what this research ought to encourage is critical self-reflection on the production of knowledge about Australia within the countries and cultures concerned. In fact, this is a dimension almost entirely lacking in Australian studies in Asia at present: Australia is 'there', China or Japan is 'here'. Much of the work is still posited in terms of opposition — China vs. Australia, Australia vs. Japan, in a more or less predictable pattern of binaries. But as far as I'm aware there has been little or no work done on the recent history of how knowledge about Australia in China or Japan has been produced, little dialectical understanding of the process or sense of an internal dialectic. Little work has been done on China's Australia or Japan's Australia, work I see as being as much a part of Australian studies — of a discipline examining its own groundings — as learning those trade figures or trying to pin down mateship or the bush legend once and for all.

Footnotes

[1] FitzGerald, Stephen. 1997. *Is Australia An Asian Country?* p.63. Sydney: Allen & Unwin.

[2] For a report at the end of this project, see Australian Studies Offshore: Time to Start Again? *Crossings*. Vol. 3. No. 1. August 1998. http://pandora.nla.gov.au/tep/13231

[3] New Australian studies programs are being pursued by the Australia–Indonesia Institute and the Australia–India Council.

10. AUSTRALIA AS MODEL OR MORAL

Alison Broinowski

Far from Australia being regarded as 'a model and a place for education', as one of the research areas in this project described it, the texts we have examined show that admiration for Australia is not as widespread as we might suppose among Chinese or Japanese commentators, even those who have sought to live or study here. Few of them unreservedly advocate that China or Japan should emulate Australia. Rather, they are often frustrated by Australians' ignorance about Asia, and the failure of Australians to appreciate or even to care about what to these writers is obvious: the inherent superiority of the ancient civilisations and modern achievements of China and Japan. This concluding chapter therefore raises again a question that other contributors have posed: who cares? Do Australians not care enough how they are perceived in two of the world's leading countries to do much about it? Do Chinese and Japanese not care about Australia, a country that is not in their league, except for what it tells them about themselves?

Among writers about Australia in Chinese and Japanese, it is true, are some whose impressions are positive, even enthusiastic. Several in both languages admire the lifestyle and the social mobility that they find in Australia. Some compliment

Australians on the country's development and its institutions. Some greatly admire Aboriginal culture. Even the admirers of Australia, however, often dilute their praise with reservations.

In Hiyama Takashi's account of his 5,000km bike ride across Australia, for example, he greatly appreciates the kindness shown to him and his friends by Australians, and praises their egalitarianism and healthy family life. But then he points to the downside: 'You could say Australians are too healthy ... What is most important to Australians is for a person to have a fun life.'[1] The implication is that for him, a fun life is becoming a bicycle fanatic — something hard that he does as a challenge, but not something to which he'll devote the rest of his life.

Similar views are expressed by many Japanese writers about Australia, including the famous author, Murakami Haruki, who visited Sydney for the Olympic Games (see Leith Morton's detailed account in Chapter 6). In *Shidonii!*, he describes young Australians revelling in unrestrained displays of patriotism, and yelling 'Oi oi oi!' at every opportunity. He interprets this as a response to the authorities' aim to promote 'a positive and cheery image' to visitors, to compensate for Australia's guilt for having been a convict colony, for having created the White Australia Policy, and for having suppressed Aborigines. He finds this expression of the new, confident national image annoying, boorish and lacking class. Australia, he warns, is close to economic crisis and the 'money-lenders' (presumably meaning Japanese) may be about to call in their debts. Yet throughout the Olympic Games in this fool's paradise, he writes, 'everyone made a great racket, drank copious amounts of beer, and sang *Waltzing Matilda* about fifty times'.[2]

Chinese observers also tend to dilute their admiration for Australia with reservations. Xiao Ying visits small schools in rural Australia and is unreservedly impressed with the cooperative atmosphere, as well as the fact that the teachers have deliberately left the city to teach there.[3] The contrast with the PRC is clearly in her mind. But another Chinese visitor to

Australia, Hong Pizhi observes a picnic in a park where parents ate, drank and talked while their small children played unsupervised, falling off bikes and chasing balls unaided. He asks, 'Would [Chinese] mothers ever let their own little emperors injure themselves like this?'[4] He admires the way Australian children develop personal independence, are self-reliant in study and get part-time jobs at an early age, but believes children should seek the advice of parents and teachers. He observes the high levels of drug addiction, criminality and homelessness among young Australians as a cautionary example to Australia and China alike.

Liang Qiyun, whose *Australia Overview* was published in 1998, and who emphasises the Britishness of Australian life and institutions, describes the social welfare and superannuation systems in positive terms. But he suggests that suburban life is primitive: 'On the weekend, most husbands go to the bush near their homes to chop firewood, while their wives stay home baking'. Do it yourself, no sophistication, is the subtext. Alcohol, he writes, is the most important part of a meal. There are never more than three courses and Australians are always surprised by the length and variety of Chinese dinners. For Liang this shows that Australians lack the taste and sophistication of Chinese.[5]

Other Japanese and Chinese writers state explicitly that Australia is definitely not a model society, although the themes they choose are similar to those chosen by writers who find some things to admire. For example, Xie Kang, a naturalised Australian resident for more than 40 years, lectures his Australian workmate on the superiority and antiquity of Chinese culture and cuisine, and recites anecdotes of how he and his friends manage to outsmart ignorant, corrupt Australian officials by means of their superior intelligence.[6] Yan Zhen, describing the origins of the gay and lesbian Mardi Gras in Sydney, notes that homosexuals in Australia have civil freedom and are not pursued by the police. He does not approve of this, adding that the extravagant street carnival is a distortion of that freedom and 'a regression of human civilisation'.[7]

Anticipating his argument, an article five years earlier about Australians and their dogs by Hong Pizhu and Zhang Dishan observes that Australians are prepared to send their parents to nursing homes, yet they take their dogs everywhere, feed them imported food and pay high vets' fees for them. A neighbour responded furiously to the writers' polite comment about her dog's high-pitched yapping: 'Piss off back to your damned country!' Their conclusion is that Australians are decadent Western barbarians, who ignorantly fail to appreciate the superiority of Chinese civilisation. Chinese would be wise not to adopt Australian ways.[8]

Japanese writers who reject Australia as a model also tend to repeat familiar themes. Murayama Kenji describes his experience of visiting Uluru as cohabiting with white 'brutes' who stuff themselves with meat, have bad table manners and dance to loud, primitive music all night. He and his compatriot, Kageyama, secluding themselves from the barbarians, speculate about who are the savages, themselves or the *hakujin*.[9] Similarly, an account in *Nichigō Press* in 1999 of the 'Melbourne Incident' of 1992 asserts that five Japanese tourists who were jailed for importing heroin were unquestionably innocent — as Australian media reports have also suggested — and blames the Australian court for failing to understand them. In spite of being provided with Japanese interpreters, the writer says, the accused tourists were reluctant to assert themselves 'for fear of becoming a burden to others'.[10] The writer, Kondo Atsushi, makes no comparison with the Japanese legal process, and pays no attention to the coverage of the case in the Australian media. But by suggesting the superior sensitivity and moral stance of the Japanese accused, the writer appeals to reassuring, customary responses among Japanese readers in Australia.

A common perception of Australians among Japanese businessmen, Kyoko Sheridan reported in 1992, is that they 'only work hard after 5pm'.[11] Making a similar comparison, Zhang Xinke remarks that while Chinese work as hard and as long as they can to maximise their income, Australians are satisfied with a rough balance of income and expenditure, and live only for the present.[12] This article from Hong Kong by Cai Lan reflects the same idea.

> In Hong Kong, everyone does five things in one day. But in Australia, you are lucky to get one done. So if you want to discuss business with an Australian, when is the best time?
>
> How is Monday morning? If you think there is no better time than the beginning of the week to get some work done, you are wrong. All Australian workers are busily chatting about their weekend ...
>
> Tuesday morning? There is a lot of Monday's work that must be cleared, they are simply too busy ...
>
> Wednesday morning? They are all planning their weekend activities. It is simply impossible to turn their mind to anything about business ...
>
> Thursday afternoon. Everyone got paid in the morning and has had an expensive meal at lunchtime with a glass of wine. It is foolish to ruin the good mood with serious business ...
>
> Friday afternoon? All of them are getting anxious rushing to the start of the weekend. They have been waiting for this for five long working days. How can one expect them to concentrate on work? ...
>
> 'Is it possible for us to have morning tea and a short talk with you on Saturday morning?' we asked.
>
> 'What? You want me to work on the weekend? Go away!'[13] (Ellipses added)

Whether or not this is an accurate characterisation of Australians, it is often repeated, reflecting a widespread view that Australia has profited less from its unearned advantages than China or Japan could have done. But it seems also to evoke doubts among Chinese and Japanese about whether the long hours they work pay off by providing them with the happy, fulfilled lives that Australians appear to have.

In these and many other extracts the project has researched and translated, Australia is represented as a country whose outstanding natural assets are scarcely matched by the talents or energies of its people. The longevity of Chinese culture, and in particular its superior cuisine, are used repeatedly by Chinese writers to put uncaring Australians in their place, or to warn them that China will soon be able to define it for them. The achievements of modern Japan, and its unique national ethos, are a subtext of Japanese writers who are irritated when Australians seem not to know what their proper place is, or even to care to find out.

Footnotes

1. Hiyama Takashi. 1980. Australia is a Free Country. In *Saikuru Yarō Chūō Toppa (My Escape to Become a Cycle Fanatic: 5,000km crossing of Australia)*. Tokyo: Rippu Shobō.
2. Murakami Haruki. 2001. *Shidonii! (Sydney!)*. Tokyo: Bungei Shunjū.
3. Xiao Ying. 1998. *Feng yu Aozhou meng (Trials and Hardship: the Australian dream)*. Beijing: Zhongguo guoji guangbo chubanshe: Xin hua shu dian jing xiao.
4. Hong Pizhu and Zhang Dishan. 1993. Aozhou ren he gou (Australians and Dogs). In *Aozhou fend quing ji shi (A Record of Australian Scenery)*. pp.26–9.
5. Liang Qiyun. 1998. *Aozhou feng qing hua (Australia Overview)*. Hong Kong: Xing dao chubanshe.
6. Xie Kang. 1983. *Travelling and Living in Australia for Forty Years*. Hong Kong: Yuan Fang.
7. Yan Zhen. 1998. Gay Mardi Gras Parade. In *Gaosu ni yi ge zhen Aozhou (I'll Tell You a Real Australia)*. pp.118–29. Beijing: Zhongguo dian ying chubanshe.
8. Hong Pizhu and Zhang Dishan, Australians and Dogs.
9. Murayama Kenji. 1978. *Kaze no, Torō no Shisha (The Wind, the Fruitless Messenger)*. Tokyo: Shūeisha.
10. Kondo Atsushi. 1999. What is the 'Melbourne Incident'? Gaoled for 7 years, Japanese who received guilty sentences in Australia. In *Nichigō Press*. pp.22–3. October 1999.
11. Kyoko Sheridan (ed.). 1992. *The Australian Economy in the Japanese Mirror*. St Lucia, Queensland: University of Queensland Press.
12. Zhang Xinke. 1995. Aozhou ren he zan bu yi yang (Australians differ from us). In *Hua ren zhi sheng (Voice of the Chinese)*, 16. pp.22–3.

Further Reference

Cai Lan. 1997. *Australia: overseas emotions*. Hong Kong: Tian di tu sho you xian gong si.

ABOUT THE EDITOR

After joining the Australian Foreign Service in 1963, Alison Broinowski lived in Japan for a total of six years, and for shorter periods in Burma, Iran, the Philippines, Jordan, South Korea, the United States of America and Mexico, working alternately as an author or as an Australian diplomat. In addition to numerous articles and reviews, her publications include seven books of fact and fiction about the Australia/Asia interface, the latest being *About Face: Asian Accounts of Australia* (Scribe, 2003) and *Howard's War* (Scribe, 2003). Since leaving the Department of Foreign Affairs and Trade, she has received a PhD in Asian Studies from The Australian National University, and has continued to lecture, write, and broadcast in Australia and abroad on Asian affairs and on cultural and political issues. She is a member of the Asian Studies Association of Australia, the Asia–Pacific Council of Macquarie University, and is co-Patron of the Asian Association of Australian Studies.

www.ingramcontent.com/pod-product-compliance
Lightning Source LLC
Chambersburg PA
CBHW050927240426
43670CB00023B/2963